The Shortcut
Cook

The Shortcut Cook

Rosie Reynolds

**Photography
by Louise Hagger**

Hardie Grant

BOOKS

**Classic recipes and
the ingenious hacks
that make them faster,
simpler and tastier**

Brunch

17

Soups and salads

37

Pork and chicken

59

Beef
and lamb

83

Fish

99

Meat-free
mains

111

Desserts

133

As a trained chef, food stylist and cookbook writer, who has worked on many books and written hundreds of recipes, my job often depends on getting great food ready as fast as possible. Over the years, I've developed ways to cook meals without sacrificing taste, look and freshness. I am well placed to enlighten fellow meal-makers on the joys of taking shortcuts in order to get food on the table that not only tastes great, but looks great, too.

I was lucky enough to go to culinary school. It was an amazing but intense experience, and at times the way things were done blew my mind. For a start, we worked in a very confined space: two people shared just over 1 m (3 ft) of work surface, and we each had the use of two stove burners and half an oven. I couldn't believe I'd paid all that money to be squashed in as though I was on a caravanning holiday. With hindsight, what I now know is that it equipped me to work in any given environment, not just a fancy, high-tech professional kitchen or location house.

Chefs and kitchen professionals have always used shortcuts to create great food. Home cooks have not always been allowed the same privilege and are often made to feel guilty about using certain tricks and ingredients. This book is about using shortcuts and creative solutions to get the best food – whipped up quickly, in the best way possible – for your family. I've tried to put myself into the shoes of those who will pick this book up and ask: 'Would I like those? Would I cook from this? Would serving this give me delight and make me feel proud? Are the recipes and instructions clear?'

This book is about food and its preparation. It is intended for home cooks who want a straightforward, practical approach to preparing delicious, beautiful food without pretence. It'll give you permission to use your microwave, to use store-bought bits 'n' bobs and to use food from the freezer. It will also teach you some techniques, methods and a few unusual ingredient combos to help you achieve good-looking, great-tasting food.

There are some things that I'll always do when I'm cooking, which make my life easier, make cooking more pleasurable and help food taste its best:

+ Gather everything before you start cooking: equipment, ingredients, a clean dish towel, etc.

+ Have a large bowl or a plastic bag nearby for food waste, to keep your work station clean and clutter-free.

+ Fill the sink with hot soapy water to keep your hands clean and to speedily wash up used or dirty bowls and equipment for quick re-use. Keep a clean cloth close by for wiping and some paper towels for patting, drying and draining foods.

+ Start your cooking sessions by putting on the kettle – this will mean you can make up stock from cubes quickly, rinse out tins to add the liquid to sauces and stews, or get pasta on the boil much quicker.

+ Most pastas don't need to cook in a huge pot of boiling water, they will cook just as well in a smaller pan. Doing this will also give you an intensely starchy cooking water, which will thicken your sauces much more successfully. The same goes for boiling vegetables: you don't need huge vats of water to cook veg just a pan that's fit for purpose.

+ Make sure meat is not fridge-cold when you put it in the oven, as it will take a good 20–30 minutes to warm through before it can start cooking.

+ Like meat, eggs need to come to room temperature before cooking. This will prevent them curdling cake mixes or being undercooked when boiled.

+ Sharp knives will speed things up in the kitchen; a speed peeler will thinly and evenly slice; and a good pair of kitchen scissors will snip precisely.

+ Start seasoning your food. Taste when you're cooking (as long as it is safe to do so), then use a fine sea salt to season before and during cooking. Only use a flaky sea salt once food is cooked. If you need to check seasoning, remove a small amount of food from the pan and taste it, then add a tiny sprinkle of salt and taste again. If it tastes better with the salt, then add seasoning to the whole dish.

+ Make dressing in the salad bowl you're serving it in, then you won't have an extra bowl to wash up.

+ Herbs: Store your herbs in a glass of cold water or wrap them in paper towels and cling film (plastic wrap) and store in the refrigerator (except basil, which will go black). They will last so much longer and stay perky.

+ Find your local bay tree or rosemary bush and ask the owner nicely if you can help yourself!

+ As good food is so much more than just something to fill your belly, look at it as a whole and ask yourself: does it tick all the boxes I want it to tick?

1. Taste: Is it sweet, sour, salty, umami, creamy, savoury?
2. Texture: Is it soft, silky, crisp, dry, moist?
3. Appearance: Does it look delicious and inviting? Who am I cooking for? Can I make it look better?
4. Delivery/presentation: What will I serve it on or with? Plates or bowls? Knives and forks or spoons? Will there be bread or add-ons?

+ Be experimental – make recipes your own. Find flavour combos that work for you.

+ Finally, for washing away stuck-on grime use a little laundry washing powder – the detergent breaks down grease effectively and quickly.

Your kitchen equipment doesn't need to be fancy, or necessarily what would be used in a restaurant. But you do need some good basics and they will serve you for a long time. Like many of my recipes, I really do like to keep it simple. Here is a list of equipment that you will find useful for making the recipes in this book:

Large, sharp knife	For chopping. Invest in a good knife that you feel comfortable using. Far from being unsafe, a properly sharp knife speeds up chopping and is actually safer than using a smaller, blunt knife. Keep your knives sharp and store them on their own, not in a drawer with other utensils as this will blunt the edges.
Serrated knife	For cutting fruit, slicing cakes and halving bread rolls.
Bread knife	Essential for cutting large loaves of bread and great for halving big cakes.
Mixing bowls	A selection of sizes.
Saucepans	A selection of sizes and types. My preference is for a heavy-based pan. Small ones can be used for melting butter, poaching eggs and reheating individual portions of soup, for example. Medium-sized can be used for boiling small quantities of pasta and cooking vegetables and large ones are ideal for big stews.
Large shallow casserole dish (Dutch oven)	Choose one that works on the stove and in the oven.
Large cast-iron frying pan (skillet)	The most versatile piece of equipment that can be used on the stove and in the oven.
Ovenproof dishes	In a variety of sizes – earthenware, tin, enamel and Pyrex glass dishes all work well.
Baking trays (pans)	Get a selection – some flat sheets for all-round heat circulation and some high-sided, lipped trays for longer cooking. Make sure the trays fit in your oven.
Cake tins (pans)	20 cm/8 in round cake tin, 20 cm/8 in square brownie pan and a 900 g/2 lb loaf tin.
Digital scales	For accuracy in cooking, especially baking.

Set of measuring spoons	Ranging from ¼ teaspoon to 1 tablespoon.
Measuring jug	Essential for liquids and mixing stock cubes.
Mixing spoons and spatulas	You'll need a couple of good-quality, long-handled wooden spoons, a large metal spoon for stirring, a slotted spoon, a spatula for flipping, a palette knife for transferring and – my favourite – a rubber spatula (just make sure it's heatproof).
Chopping boards	I love a large wooden chopping board, so easy to use and easy to clean. Plastic boards also work. When buying a chopping board, choose one that you can pick up easily and is stable enough to lie flat on your work surface.
Microwave	Ideal for reheating and quick cooking.
Food processor and hand-held blender (stick blender)	Good for chopping things quickly and making silky smooth soups.
Hand-held electric whisk or balloon whisk	For whipping and whisking in minutes.
Box grater and precision grater	The latter is useful for grating things like garlic, ginger and Parmesan.
Speed peeler and julienne peeler	I use these two all the time, especially when making salads.
Kitchen scissors	A good strong pair – I use mine for everything from snipping herbs to chopping bacon directly into the pan.
Rolling pin	For rolling out pastry and bashing things into crumbs.
Oven thermometer and sugar (pan) thermometer	For accuracy in the oven and when frying.
Chef's blowtorch	For bruléeing and browning.

Sauces, pastes and preserved goods

+ soy sauce
+ fish sauce
+ miso
+ chilli sauces (Sriracha and sweet chilli)
+ rice vinegar
+ curry paste
+ crispy fried onions
+ Marmite (yeast extract)
+ stock cubes
+ anchovies, mustard(s)
+ hot sauce
+ red wine vinegar
+ white wine vinegar
+ cider vinegar

Oils

+ light olive oil
+ extra virgin olive oil
+ sesame oil
+ a light-flavoured oil, such as vegetable, sunflower or rapeseed (canola)

Spice rack

+ thyme
+ rosemary
+ fennel seeds
+ dried chilli (hot pepper) flakes
+ Turkish pepper flakes
+ ground and whole cumin seeds
+ ground coriander
+ ground turmeric
+ ground cinnamon
+ mixed spice
+ garam masala
+ cardamom pods
+ cayenne pepper
+ paprika
+ nutmeg
+ black pepper
+ Chinese five spice

Salt

+ fine sea salt or crystal kosher salt (for seasoning food before and during cooking)
+ flaky sea salt (for seasoning finished dishes)

Sugars and sweeteners

+ caster (superfine) sugar
+ demerara sugar
+ soft light brown sugar
+ soft dark brown sugar
+ icing (confectioner's) sugar
+ maple syrup
+ honey

Flours and baking goods

+ plain (all-purpose) flour
+ gluten-free flour
+ cornflour (cornstarch)
+ baking powder
+ bicarbonate of soda (baking soda)
+ cream of tartar
+ xanthan gum

Tinned goods

+ assorted beans
+ chickpeas (garbanzo beans)
+ tomatoes
+ coconut milk
+ evaporated milk
+ tuna fish
+ anchovies

Dried goods

+ assorted pasta (spaghetti, a short pasta such as penne, and orzo or a soup pasta)
+ risotto rice
+ basmati rice
+ egg noodles
+ rice noodles/vermicelli
+ croutons

I find it helpful to plan what I am going to be eating for the next two to three days. I make a shopping list and (try) to stick to it, buying all of the fresh ingredients and any dry goods I know I will need to make the recipes. Doing this helps me: 1. stay focused on eating good food; 2. not have a refrigerator full of random ingredients and no idea what to cook; and 3. minimise waste.

Store fresh and dry ingredients according to the manufacturer's instructions. Fresh fruit and veg will stay fresher longer in the refrigerator, although tomatoes are better kept at room temperature. Mushrooms should be removed from any plastic wrapping and put into a paper bag or laid on paper towels before chilling.

Once you have cooked the recipes, store leftovers in a plastic or glass container with a lid, or on a plate or bowl covered with cling film (plastic wrap) or kitchen foil. Cakes will keep well in an airtight container or wrapped tightly in cling film or kitchen foil.

I love an organised freezer – not only does it mean I can stock it with frozen meals and raw ingredients, it also means the food is easy to access and rotate (minimising food waste and damage from the dreaded freezer burn).

Freezer burn is the accumulation of ice molecules that look like white-coloured frozen fuzz on your food. This happens when the moisture inside the food travels into the space between the food and the surrounding air and freezes on the food's surface. Not only does it look awful, but it actually changes the texture of your food and causes it to dry out. It can also affect the taste.

There are a few things you can do to minimise damage from freezer burn and keep your food looking, tasting and feeling great:

Press cling film directly over the surface of the food to stop the air getting to it and spoiling it. Try it with ice cream – I am sure you have experienced that horrible gummy ice cream with masses of ice crystals at the top of your favourite frozen treat. Now you know what it is and can work to prevent it with this simple tip.

Put food in freezer-safe food bags and push out all of the air. The best way to do this is to not overfill the bag, then lay flat on a surface and use your fingers to gently push out all of the air while slowly sealing. You can also wrap food tightly in freezer-safe cling film. If you do decide to use plastic containers, lay a sheet of freezer-safe cling film on the surface of the food and use your fingers to gently push out any trapped air between the food and the cling film before sealing with a lid.

If possible, try to freeze your food as flat as possible. This way you can store frozen food like books on a book shelf or files in a filing cabinet. Date your frozen packages and make sure you rotate them, pulling the older stuff to the front and using it before you use any newly frozen goods. Keeping your freezer organised and easily accessible helps you know what you have available to cook with, what needs to be used and by what date.

I usually freeze food in portions of two: that way I have enough for two people or dinner for me and an extra portion for lunch. You can, of course, freeze a big batch and defrost the whole thing, then cook and serve. I often find freezing in single portions helpful, too – the food will defrost faster and it means you don't have to eat the same food for several days.

To defrost food quickly and evenly, a cool trick is to defrost on an aluminium tray. This is great for defrosting pieces of fish or meat. You can also run your frozen food under cold water, or leave it to stand in a cold water bath. Alternatively, place it on a tray in the refrigerator overnight for use the following day.

Batch cooking is a brilliant way to stay ahead in the meal-planning game. Doubling the recipe quantities means you can eat one and freeze one. I double up on recipes such as ragù, chilli, soups and stocks, and cook extra ingredients such as grains and vegetables, which I then cool and store in the refrigerator and freezer for use throughout the week. Think about those ingredients and recipes that can be used as building blocks for a great meal, i.e. a batch of frozen chilli + the sweet potatoes lying around + buying coriander and yogurt on the way home = dinner sorted.

Before freezing or chilling in the refrigerator, allow the food to cool down quickly. If chilling, you can leave it in the dish the recipe was cooked in and reheat from chilled. If freezing, decant the food into a container or wrap tightly in cling film or a freezer-safe bag, expelling any excess air before freezing.

To get the best out of the recipes, always read through the ingredients list and the method before you start cooking. This will allow you to familiarise yourself with the recipe, so you know what is coming up. I always do this every time I cook something new. It's also helpful to look at the first line of the method before you start prepping and chopping – if it says 'preheat the oven' you can do this immediately so you're ready to go!

All of the recipes have a prep time (this tells you how long it will take you to get everything ready pre-cooking) and a cook time (how long the recipe will take on the heat or in the oven). These are a guide, please use them as such.

The ingredients are listed in the order in which they appear in the recipe method, and the preparation required is listed next to the ingredient (e.g. chopped, sliced, grated, etc.). If you work your way down the ingredient list and prep the ingredients as you go, you will be ready to start cooking as soon as you reach the end of the list. There is a fancy chef term for this: *mise-en-place* (everything in its place).

The 'Shortcut' box in the bottom corner of each of the recipes highlights how this method will save you time or help you achieve a more delicious result.

The 'Make ahead' box will tell you which bits can be done in advance and if there are any freeze-able components that can be used in the recipes.

I would urge you to follow each recipe closely the first time you cook it. I know it works and love how it tastes and looks. Once you've made it once, eaten it and enjoyed it, you can then make it your own the second time around, probably introducing even more shortcuts to get to a super meal on the table for your family and friends.

Enjoy!

01

Brunch

Croque monsieur with Bloody Mary salad

Serves 4
Prep 15 minutes
Cook 25 minutes

Easily doubled

I have kept this recipe traditional, using thick-sliced smoked ham and gruyère cheese. However, if you want to mix things up a bit or you have vegetarian guests, you can layer up roasted veg, such as (bell) peppers, courgettes (zucchini) or aubergines (eggplants) – or a mix – in place of ham.

The beauty of this dish is that it is all baked in the oven – no filling and flipping individual sandwiches. The whole dish comes to the table. If you want to turn your monsieur into a madame, simply fry an egg and slide it on top.

This dish is great served with the Bloody Mary salad, but you can serve it alone if brunch is too early for salad ... And, of course, if it is too early for vodka, just leave it out: the crunchy salad will still be great with the rich, gooey croque monsieur.

8 slices white bread
3 tablespoons butter, plus extra
    for spreading
50 g (1¾ oz) plain
    (all-purpose) flour
300 ml (10 fl oz/1¼ cups) whole
    (full-fat) milk
100 ml (3½ fl oz) double
    (heavy) cream
4 egg yolks
1½ tablespoons Dijon mustard
nutmeg, for grating
4 slices good-quality ham
    (I used hand-carved ham)
200 g (7 oz) gruyère cheese,
    grated
sea salt and freshly ground
    black pepper

For the Bloody Mary salad

200 g (7 oz) ripe tomatoes,
    roughly chopped
2 celery sticks, sliced
¼ teaspoon celery salt
2 tablespoons olive oil
1 shot of ice-cold vodka
squeeze of lemon juice
Tabasco sauce, to taste
sea salt and freshly ground
    black pepper

Preheat the oven to 200°C/180°C Fan/400°F/Gas 6. Place a roasting tray (pan) measuring roughly 30 x 20 cm (12 x 8 in) in the oven to heat up.

Spread the bread slices with butter. Lay 4 slices buttered-side down in the tray and top with the remaining 4 slices, buttered-side up. Cook in the oven for 5 minutes, or until the bread is crisp and turning golden. Remove from the oven.

Meanwhile, make the béchamel. Put the butter, flour and milk in a small pan set over a medium heat and stir continuously until you have a smooth, thick sauce. Remove from the heat and stir in the cream, egg yolks, mustard and a grating of nutmeg. Return to the heat and cook, stirring continuously, until the sauce is thick – this will take 2–3 minutes. Season to taste.

Lift the top 4 slices of bread out of the tray and spread 2 tablespoons of béchamel over the bottom 4 slices of bread. Cover with ham, scatter over half of the gruyère, add a dollop more of béchamel, then sandwich with the remaining bread, toasted-side up. Cover the whole dish generously with the remaining béchamel and gruyère. Bake for 10–15 minutes, or until golden and bubbling.

To make the Bloody Mary salad, mix all the ingredients except the Tabasco in a bowl. Taste for seasoning and add a dash of of Tabasco to taste before serving.

Make ahead

The béchamel will keep in an airtight container in the refrigerator for at least 2–3 days.

The shortcut

The one-step béchamel saves a good 15 minutes. Cooking four sandwiches in one go means no standing at the stove and production-line service for your guests.

Breakfast nachos

Serves 4
Prep 15 minutes
Cook 10 minutes

My breakfast nachos are essentially fried corn tortillas cooked in a spicy sauce. Think warm, saucy nachos. Instead of frying up fresh corn tortillas, in this recipe I use store-bought salted corn tortilla chips, meaning the dish can be whipped up in minutes. The beauty of this recipe is the combination of both crunchy and soft sauce-soaked tortillas, dunked into a fried egg. I add a couple of anchovy fillets to the base for an umami kick – it's not traditional, but it really builds in flavour when you are making a quick sauce.

Half the base salsa is cooked out with stock and used to coat the tortillas and the other half is used as a fresh raw salsa, which provides a great kick to the dish and textural contrast.

This can be made in minutes, and is a great dish to serve family style for everyone to dig in. Don't be surprised if it moves from a brunch staple to a weeknight supper.

2 garlic cloves, roughly chopped
1 red onion, roughly chopped
1 red chilli, roughly chopped
2 anchovy fillets, roughly chopped
1 tablespoon red wine vinegar
3 roasted red (bell) peppers from
    a jar, drained and chopped
3 ripe plum tomatoes, deseeded
    and roughly chopped
3 tablespoons olive oil, plus
    an extra drizzle
200 ml (7 fl oz/¾ cup) hot
    chicken or vegetable stock
175 g (6 oz) bag lightly salted
    tortilla chips
4 eggs

To serve
1 large avocado, chopped (optional)
sour cream
handful of coriander (cilantro),
    chopped

Put the garlic, onion, chilli, anchovies, vinegar, peppers, tomatoes and 2 tablespoons of the oil into the bowl of a food processor, and pulse a couple of times to bring everything together, creating a salsa. Tip half of the salsa into a bowl and set aside.

Whizz the remaining salsa until smooth.

Heat 1 tablespoon of oil in a large deep saucepan set over a medium–high heat and fry the smooth salsa for 2 minutes. Stir in the stock and continue to cook for 5 minutes, or until thickened slightly. Add the tortilla chips and carefully fold to coat in the sauce. Cook for a further 3 minutes or until the chips are warm.

Meanwhile, heat a drizzle of oil in a large non-stick frying pan (skillet) over a medium heat, crack in the eggs and fry to your liking.

Divide the tortilla chips between 4 plates and slide a fried egg on to each one. Add some avocado, if using, along with sour cream and coriander, and serve immediately with the remaining chunky salsa.

Make ahead

The salsa can be made in advance and kept in the fridge for 2 days, stored in an airtight container.

The shortcut

No deep-frying! Opening a packet, in this instance, is a worthy time – and mess-saver that's guaranteed to add to your enjoyment of the dish.

Eggs Benedict

Serves 2
Prep 10 minutes
Cook 8 minutes

Easily doubled

I think we can all agree that the most important part of eggs Benedict is the hollandaise – the rich, buttery sauce that has such a bad reputation for being difficult to make. Well, I make my hollandaise in the microwave – it's super quick and really easy and it works every time. Make sure your yolks are large!

Poach your eggs in advance, cool and reheat in a pan of boiling water for 30 seconds or so, then assemble and serve. Toast your muffins and keep them warm in the oven while you make your sauce.

1½ tablespoons white wine vinegar
4 large eggs
2 English muffins
butter, for spreading
4 slices of good-quality ham

For the hollandaise
75 g (2½ oz/¼ cup) butter
2 large egg yolks
¼ teaspoon white wine vinegar
2 teaspoons lemon juice
2 tablespoons hot water
sea salt and freshly ground
    black pepper

Bring a small deep saucepan of water to the boil over a high heat and add 1 tablespoon of the vinegar. Pour the remaining vinegar into 4 ramekins or small glasses and swirl to coat the insides with vinegar, then tip out the excess. Crack an egg into each ramekin. Swirl the boiling water to form a vortex, then slide 1 egg from its ramekin into the middle of the swirling water and cook for 3 minutes. Remove with a slotted spoon. Repeat with the remaining eggs, one at a time, re-swirling the water as before and sliding the egg in.

Meanwhile, split and toast the muffins and spread with butter. Put the muffin halves on 2 serving plates, and top each half with a slice of ham and a poached egg. Keep warm.

For the hollandaise, put the butter in a small microwave-safe jug and heat in the microwave for 15–20 seconds, or until melted. Beat together the egg yolks, vinegar, lemon juice and hot water in a separate microwave-safe bowl until smooth. Season well, then gradually pour the melted butter into this mixture, whisking continuously to incorporate. Heat in the microwave in 15-second bursts for 1 minute, whisking between each burst until the hollandaise is thick and smooth.

Pour the hollandaise over the poached eggs and serve immediately.

Make ahead

Poach your eggs up to 3 hours ahead – cook as above, then plunge into an ice bath. Reheat the eggs in a pan of boiling water for 30 seconds before serving.

The shortcut

Making the hollandaise in the microwave will save you a good 10 minutes, plus this method means it's much less likely to split, saving hours of heartache.

Brunch

Scrambled egg tacos

Serves 4
Prep 10 minutes
Cook 10 minutes

I like my scrambled eggs to run a fine line between scrambled eggs and, well, a just-set savoury, creamy custard. To make my eggs light and fluffy, I add a pinch of baking powder to the egg mixture before cooking.

I love these breakfast tacos; they look great and can be made in a matter of minutes. I make a lightly spiced *pico de gallo* to scatter over the top with some hot sauce. The fresh tomato, onion and coriander (cilantro) is the perfect foil to the rich, creamy eggs.

I've said it before and I'll say it again, nobody is watching, so add whatever you like to your breakfast taco – it's YOURS!

I want mine with crispy prosciutto.

8 small flour or corn tortillas
8 eggs, lightly beaten
200 ml (7 fl oz/scant 1 cup)
    double (heavy) cream
¼ teaspoon baking powder
1 teaspoon fine sea salt
1 tablespoon butter

For the pico de gallo

4 ripe tomatoes, halved,
    deseeded and chopped
½ onion, finely chopped
handful of coriander (cilantro),
    finely chopped
1 green chilli, deseeded and
    finely chopped
juice of ½ lime
sea salt and freshly ground
    black pepper

To serve

1 avocado, halved, stoned
    and sliced
hot sauce
lime wedges (optional)

To make the pico de gallo, mix the tomatoes, onion, coriander and chilli in a bowl. Season to taste and squeeze over the lime juice. Set aside.

Using a pair of tongs, carefully hold a tortilla over an open gas flame until hot and blackened in places. Keep the tortilla warm while you cook the rest (I wrap my tortillas in a clean dish towel).

In a bowl, whisk the eggs, cream, baking powder and salt until fully combined.

Melt the butter in a large, non-stick frying pan (skillet) over a medium–high heat. Pour in the egg mixture and cook until just set around the edge of the pan. Push the egg from around the edge into the middle, then tilt the pan and allow the uncooked egg to run to the edge. Keep repeating this process. When the eggs are just set, spoon them on top of the charred tortillas and serve immediately with slices of avocado, pico de gallo, hot sauce and lime wedges.

Make ahead

Pico de gallo can be made in advance and stored in the fridge for a couple of days.

The shortcut

Adding a generous helping of cream ensures the tastiest, softest eggs and adding that pinch of baking powder makes them fluffy without the need to whisk.

Brunch

Devilled eggs

Serves 4
Prep 15, minutes
plus chilling
Cook 10 minutes

Easily doubled

You will hear me say this often, but even if I don't go to the effort of cooking every offering from scratch, when I am hosting I like to make at least one thing for my guests that will guarantee high praise: something that looks great and can be mixed in with other bits and bobs to create a visual and tasty treat. Devilled eggs are the perfect shortcut star of the show – quick to make and delicious to eat.

The trick to great devilled eggs begins before you even cook them – take them out of the refrigerator and bring them to room temperature. This will stop them cracking in the hot water. To further reduce cracking, use a pan just big enough to fit your eggs snugly, so they don't roll around.

I use a combination of mayonnaise, very soft butter and pickle juice with my egg yolks. The butter lends a rich, luxurious texture and taste, while the mayo offers its cool creamy flavour to the eggs, and the pickle vinegar cuts through the richness, which I love because it means I can eat more. And don't worry if they don't look pretty – cover with a pinch of cayenne and some chopped chives.

1 teaspoon fine sea salt
6 large eggs (at room temperature)
3 tablespoons good-quality
mayonnaise
1 tablespoon butter,
well softened
1 teaspoon Dijon mustard
1 teaspoon juice from a jar of
pickles, or white wine vinegar
cayenne pepper, for sprinkling
1 tablespoon finely
chopped chives
sea salt and freshly ground
black pepper

Bring a medium saucepan of water and a pinch of salt to the boil over a medium–high heat. Use a large spoon to carefully lower the eggs into the water and cook for 10 minutes.

Meanwhile, fill a large bowl with cold water and ice. Lift the cooked eggs out and immediately submerge them in the ice-cold water so they cool quickly. Alternatively, hold them under cold running water until completely cool.

Holding an egg with your fingertips, tap it hard on the work surface then roll it under your hand to crack the egg all the way around. Peel off the shell, starting at the fattest end of the egg. Repeat until you have peeled all the eggs.

Halve the eggs and use a teaspoon to scoop the yolks into a small bowl. Mash the yolks with a fork, then stir through the mayonnaise, butter, mustard and pickle juice or vinegar, and season with salt and pepper. Check the flavour and add more of any of the ingredients to suit your taste.

Spoon the filling into a small, strong sandwich bag, then leave in the fridge for 15 minutes to firm up. Snip the corner off the bag and pipe the yolk mixture into the whites.

Arrange the eggs on a plate, dust with a little cayenne pepper and sprinkle with the chives just before serving.

Make ahead

Hard-boil your eggs up to 5 days in advance, then cool and leave in the shells until ready to prepare. The yolk mixture can be prepared a day ahead before piping into the whites.

The shortcut

Spooning your egg yolk filling into a sandwich bag and snipping off the corner to fill your whites save a good 15 minutes fiddling with piping (pastry) bags and nozzles.

Brunch

Brunch traybake

Serves 4
Prep 10 minutes
Cook 40 minutes

It is often the way that the most simple-sounding food can be the most complicated to get right. For me, the 'full English' can go so wrong, and it's because timing everything so that it's cooked and delivered to perfection is just so tricky. This single-tray full English takes the pain out of preparing breakfast for a crowd. It also reduces the washing-up, which means starting your day on the right note. The beauty of a one-pan English breakfast is that all of the flavours get the chance to meld together, so increasing their own deliciousness. My favourite part is the bread cooked under the bacon and sausage – accidental (or not) fried bread.

olive oil, for drizzling
8 good-quality sausages
8 dry-cured smoked
 bacon rashers
4 portobello mushrooms,
 stalks trimmed
200 g (7 oz) cherry vine tomatoes,
 cut into small bunches
4 slices black pudding (optional)
4 slices sourdough bread
4 large eggs
200 g (7 oz) bag spinach leaves
1 tablespoon water
1 small garlic clove, grated

Preheat the oven to 200°C/180°C Fan/400°F/Gas 6.

Drizzle a little oil over a large baking tray (pan), then add the sausages and cook in the oven for 10 minutes. Add the bacon to the tray, then return to the oven for another 15 minutes.

Remove the tray from the oven and add the mushrooms, tomatoes and black pudding. Drizzle the bread with a little oil and lay, oiled-side down, underneath the sausages and bacon. Cook everything for 10 minutes.

Make 4 spaces in the ingredients and crack in the eggs. Cook for a further 5–8 minutes, or until done to your liking.

Meanwhile, open the bag of spinach and add the water and grated garlic to the bag. Cook it in the microwave for 1 minute, or until wilted. Tip the spinach into a bowl and drizzle with olive oil. Bring the full English tray to the table and let everybody help themselves.

Make ahead

Get everything ready the night before: slice your bread, snip tomatoes into bunches and set the table ready for friends.

The shortcut

A single roasting pan versus 3–4 frying pans (skillets), plus the oven on to keep things warm ... this shortcut is a no-brainer. Cooking spinach in the bag takes a minute, and means no washing up.

Brunch

The best French toast ever

Serves 6
Prep 15 minutes, plus 20 minutes or overnight soaking
Cook 30 minutes

Wow, I love French toast! There is just so much to love – the myriad of different textures in one dish: crisp, soft, fluffy, crunchy. Not to mention the flavours, from sweet to salty. It has it all. What I am not so keen on is all that dipping and flipping. When I make brunch, I want to sit down with my guests and enjoy the food at the same time, not 20 minutes later when everyone else has eaten. This one-dish French toast is perfect for feeding a crowd. It can be made ahead and left to sit overnight in the refrigerator, ready for baking the following day. No separate frying bacon and no extra pan to wash. The smoky bacon-and-pecan-nut topping and the final flourish of cinnamon sugar is just genius – as they cook, the bacon fat flavours the crisp nuts. This would also work on good vanilla ice cream – just saying.

butter, for greasing
6 large eggs
200 ml (7 fl oz/scant 1 cup) milk
200 ml (7 fl oz/scant 1 cup) double (heavy) cream
4 tablespoons caster (superfine) sugar
2 teaspoons vanilla extract
½ teaspoon mixed spice
¼ teaspoon salt
500 g (1 lb 2 oz) sourdough loaf (or white bread or brioche), cut into 2.5 cm (1 in) cubes
200 g (7 oz/1⅓ cups) blueberries
maple syrup, to serve

For the crunchy topping

90 g (3¼ oz/scant ⅔ cup) smoked bacon lardons, finely chopped
handful of pecan nuts, roughly chopped
1 tablespoon caster (superfine) sugar
1 teaspoon ground cinnamon
pinch of mixed spice

Grease a 20 x 30 cm (8 x 12 in) baking dish with butter.

In a bowl or jug, mix the eggs, milk, cream, sugar, vanilla extract, mixed spice and salt. Put half of the bread cubes in the baking dish, and pour over half of the egg mixture, pushing down with your fingers to make sure the bread is soaked. Scatter over half of the blueberries. Cover with the remaining bread cubes, egg mixture and blueberries. Cover the dish with cling film (plastic wrap) and chill in the refrigerator for 20 minutes, or even overnight, while the bread soaks.

Preheat the oven to 180°C/160°C Fan/350°F/Gas 4.

Remove and discard the cling film from the dish. Scatter the chopped bacon over the top and bake for 20 minutes. Mix the rest of the crunchy topping ingredients together, sprinkle over the French toast and return to the oven for 10 more minutes, or until the egg mixture is set and puffy and the nuts are toasty.

Serve with maple syrup.

Make ahead

This can sit in the refrigerator for up to 24 hours. The bacon-and-nut topping can be prepped and kept in an airtight container in the refrigerator for 2 days.

The shortcut

With no 'dip and flip', and no additional bowl for that purpose, you save on washing-up as well as cooking time with the big-batch approach.

Quick and easy cinnamon buns

Makes	12
Prep	20 minutes
Cook	20 minutes, plus
	30 minutes cooling

I haven't gone so far as to time it, but I do think these buns can be whipped up in the time it would take you to get your sleepy self along to a bakery to pick up a few for brunch.

Unlike most cinnamon buns, these are not made with a yeasted bread base, so there's no waiting around while the dough rises, or struggling to shape a dough that can sometimes be unruly; just a quick mix and a pat out of a very co-operative dough and you're on your way to heaven.

150 g (5 oz/scant ⅔ cup) butter, plus extra for greasing
100 g (3½ oz/generous ¾ cup) icing (confectioner's) sugar, sifted
½ teaspoon vanilla bean paste or extract
1 tablespoon boiling water
250 ml (8½ fl oz/1 cup) buttermilk
2 teaspoons ground cinnamon
¼ teaspoon mixed spice
75 g (2½ oz/scant ½ cup) soft light brown sugar
25 g (1 oz/2 tablespoons) caster (superfine) sugar
300 g (10½ oz/2½ cups) plain (all-purpose) flour, plus extra for dusting
1 teaspoon baking powder
½ teaspoon bicarbonate of soda (baking soda)
fine salt

Melt the butter in a small pan or in a bowl in the microwave. Lightly grease a large baking tray (pan) with the extra butter.

To make the glaze, mix 3 tablespoons of the melted butter in a bowl with the icing sugar and vanilla paste. Add the boiling water and 2 tablespoons of the buttermilk and stir to combine. Cover and chill.

To make the cinnamon filling, mix 3 tablespoons of the melted butter with the cinnamon, mixed spice and both types of sugar. Add a pinch of salt, then stir the mixture together until it resembles wet sand. Set aside.

Preheat the oven to 200°C/180°C Fan/400°F/Gas 6.

To make the dough, combine the flour, baking powder and bicarbonate of soda in a mixing bowl and add a generous pinch of salt. Make a well in the middle of the mixture and pour in the remaining melted butter and the rest of the buttermilk. Stir with a rubber spatula until fully combined. The dough might seem dry, but keep stirring until the dry ingredients absorb the wet – the dough will be shaggy, not smooth, at this point.

Tip the dough out on to a lightly floured work surface and knead for 3–4 minutes. When ready, the dough will look smooth and have a slight shine, and you will feel it is more elastic. Flour the work surface again and pat the dough out to a rough 20 x 30 cm (8 x 12 in) rectangle. Sprinkle the filling in an even layer over the dough, leaving a rough 1 cm (½ in) border. Press the filling into the dough. Roll up the dough lengthways up as tightly as you can, to form a long sausage shape. Cut into 12 equal pieces.

Transfer the buns to the prepared tray, cut-side up, leaving about 2 cm (¾ in) between each. Bake for 20 minutes or until puffed up, golden and sticky. Cool for 30 minutes, then remove the glaze from the refrigerator and spread over the buns. Serve immediately or let the glaze set.

Make ahead

Make the glaze first and leave it to stand in the refrigerator. As the glaze cools, the butter begins to set and thicken, so it resembles a cream-cheese frosting. Make the buns a day ahead and reheat in the oven without the glaze.

The shortcut

No yeast translates to 1½ hours of your life back. You're welcome. Pat the dough out; don't bother dirtying your rolling pin.

Brunch

Nutty granola with strained yoghurt

Serves	4, with leftover granola
Prep	10 minutes
Cook	20 minutes

I love granola and eat it any time of day. I use it in place of a sweet treat if I am being 'good'; as a snack with a drink, sprinkled with salt and chilli flakes; as an energy bar substitute; as a trail mix; to top Greek yoghurt as a pudding; and, of course, for breakfast with ice-cold milk.

Making your own granola can be cheaper than store-bought and it means you can tailor it to your personal tastes. I don't like loads of dried fruit and I like my nuts toasty and dark. I love crunchy clusters and a sweet–savoury flavour profile.

The great thing about this recipe is that you can swap in and out your favourite nuts and seeds, dried fruit and even grains. I've used traditional oats, but quinoa and buckwheat would be good, too. There is no refined sugar and the nut butter creates an extra-specially crunchy, tasty exterior to the granola.

If you ever have granola bowls in restaurants, you may notice that the yoghurt is always deliciously thick. There is a simple trick you can use to achieve this: just strain the yoghurt through a clean cloth or some paper towels. Not essential, but workth it for that luxury restaurant touch.

500 g (1 lb 2 oz/2 cups) Greek yoghurt
light-flavoured oil, for greasing
4 tablespoons natural, sugar-free, salt-free smooth nut butter (I use almond)
100 ml (3½ fl oz/scant ½ cup) maple syrup, plus extra to serve
3 tablespoons hot water
¼ teaspoon salt
150 g (5 oz/1 cup) almonds, roughly chopped
150 g (5 oz/1¼ cups) pecans, roughly chopped
150 g (5 oz/1 cup) mixed seeds
100 g (3½ oz/1 cup) rolled oats
1 teaspoon ground cinnamon
¼ teaspoon mixed spice
50 g (2 oz/⅓ cup) dried cranberries
fresh fruit, to serve (I like strawberries)

Line a sieve (strainer) with several pieces of paper towel and set it over a large mixing bowl. Tip the yoghurt into the sieve and pull up the edges of the paper towel to contain the yoghurt. Twist the ends and leave to drain.

Preheat the oven to 180°C/160°C Fan/350°F/Gas 4. Lightly grease a large baking tray (pan).

Mix the nut butter, maple syrup and hot water with the salt, and stir until combined.

Toss the nuts, seeds, oats and spices together in a large bowl, then pour over the wet ingredients and stir to coat. Spread the granola out in an even layer on the baking tray. Bake for 25 minutes, stirring every 8 minutes, until the nuts are golden and fragrant.

Stir in the dried cranberries and allow to cool completely.

Serve the granola with a scoop of the strained yoghurt and some fresh fruit.

Store the granola in an airtight container for up to 1 month.

Make ahead

The granola will keep well in an airtight container for up to 1 month. You could also prep the wet mix 1–2 days in advance and toss with the dry ingredients at the last minute.

The shortcut

Hot water and nut butter magically meld together, meaning no need to melt ingredients together.

Brunch

02

Soups

salads

A really good stock

Makes about 2 litres
(70 fl oz/8 cups)
Prep 10 minutes
Cook 1 hour

This stock is so simple and yields a really tasty stock that can be used as the base of soups, risottos and sauces. I like using good quality chicken wings – they're cheap, readily available and taste great. They're also packed full of collagen for a lovely viscous stock and covered in skin with a nice amount of fat, which is guaranteed to add flavour to the finished stock.

Browning the wings at the beginning of cooking intensifies the chicken flavour, and using chicken stock cubes, which admittedly might feel wrong in a homemade stock, has a double concentrate effect. Don't bother peeling your veggies – scrub off any dirt then chop. Leaving the onions unpeeled adds a rich brown colour to your stock, and is a top chef trick.

olive oil
750 g (1 lb 10 oz) chicken wings
2 unpeeled onions, quartered
1 large carrot, roughly chopped
1 celery stalk, roughly chopped
2 tablespoons olive oil
2 bay leaves
5 thyme sprigs
1 teaspoon black peppercorns

2 chicken stock cubes
2 litres (70 fl oz/8 cups)
very warm water
1 teaspoon sea salt flakes

Heat a drizzle of oil in a large, high-sided saucepan over a medium-high heat. Add the chicken in a single layer, skin-side down, and cook, without touching for 10 minutes. Flip over and cook for further 5 minutes. (After the first ten minutes, the chicken will have self-released and the skin should not be stuck to the pan).

Add the remaining ingredients, except the stock cubes, water and sea salt, to the pan. Stir to mix everything together.

Dissolve the stock cubes in the water add to the pan, bring to a rolling boil then reduce the heat so the stock gently bubbles. Partially cover with a lid and simmer for 45 minutes.

Remove from the heat, half fill your sink with cold water and plunge the hot pan into the water – this will cool the stock down quickly. Strain the cooled stock through a sieve and push as much of the goodness into the stock as you can, stir in the sea salt. Chill until required.

Make ahead

This is absolutely one to have up your sleeve, or rather in the freezer, for up to a month.

The shortcut

Not peeling your veg and roughly chopping saves you a good 10 minutes. Wings cook in a fraction of the time of whole chickens, so you get your stock ready sooner.

Pea velouté

Serves	4
Prep	5 minutes
Cook	15 minutes

I had you at velouté, didn't I?

It's quite nice to use such a beautiful French word to describe what is the most simple of soups. Velouté simply means 'velvety', and velvety is just how I like my pea soups. My mum would make old-fashioned pea soup using soaked dried peas, cooked for hours on end until they broke down into a creamy, smooth mass. Well, I am happy to report you don't need to soak, or cook, peas for hours. This soup can be on the table in 20 minutes from beginning to end.

Starting the soup off with a roux and adding a tin of white beans and their liquid creates that all-important smooth, velvety texture. The protein in the bean water thickens the soup, while the beans bring the creaminess.

Make this vegan by dropping the butter and doubling up on the olive oil; or make it meaty by frying up some smoked bacon with the onions – both options work wonderfully.

2 tablespoons butter
1 tablespoon olive oil, plus extra
    to serve
6 spring onions (scallions),
    chopped
1 fresh or dried bay leaf
2 tablespoons plain
    (all-purpose) flour
800 ml (27 fl oz/3¼ cups) hot
    good-quality vegetable
    or chicken stock
500 g (1 lb 2 oz/3⅓ cups)
    frozen peas
400 g (14 oz) tin butter (lima) beans
handful of mint leaves, roughly
    chopped, plus extra to serve
sea salt and freshly ground
    black pepper
pinch of chilli (hot pepper)
    flakes, to serve (optional)
crusty bread, to serve

Heat the butter and olive oil in a large saucepan over a medium heat. Once the butter is foaming, add the spring onions and bay leaf, and fry gently for 5 minutes until the onion is soft but without colour. Stir in the flour and cook for 2 minutes, then gradually add the hot stock, stirring continuously until smooth.

Add the peas to the pan, along with the beans and the liquid from the tin. Bring to the boil, then reduce the heat and simmer for 3–5 minutes, or until the peas are tender.

Stir in the chopped mint and plenty of salt and pepper, then use a hand-held (stick) blender to blend the soup until completely smooth.

Ladle into bowls, scatter with mint leaves and add a drizzle of olive oil and a pinch of chilli flakes, if using. Serve with plenty of crusty bread alongside.

Make ahead

An excellent one for the freezer for cold winter nights, this will keep well for a good while in the freezer and for up to 2 days in the refrigerator.

The shortcut

With all the soaking usually required, you're saving in excess of 24 hours here. Adding beans gives a creamy, luxurious quality without the need for extra ingredients, such as cream.

Soups and salads

French onion soup

Serves 4
Prep 10 minutes
Cook 30 minutes

Easily doubled
Soup can be frozen

4 large onions, peeled and
   very thinly sliced
4 tablespoons butter
4 tablespoons garlic-flavoured
   olive oil
pinch of bicarbonate of soda
   (baking soda)
4 sprigs of thyme
2 bay leaves
1 tablespoon cider vinegar
   or white wine vinegar
1½ tablespoons plain
   (all-purpose) flour
1 litre (34 fl oz/4 cups) good-
   quality beef or chicken stock
1 rustic baguette, sliced into
   2.5 cm (1 in) slices
200 g (7 oz) gruyère cheese,
   grated
sea salt and freshly ground
   black pepper

Traditional French onion soup can take hours to make, but this recipe will have a rich, delicious soup on the table in no time – and your kitchen sending out wafts of toasted bread and molten cheese. For me, this soup is a vehicle for eating more toasted bread, crunchy with melted cheese on top and soaked with soup underneath. I double up on the toasts so that you can re-top when you're halfway down your bowl.

Put the onions into a large microwave-safe bowl and dot half of the butter over the top. Microwave on full power for 10 minutes, stirring halfway through.

Melt the remaining butter and 1 tablespoon of the garlic oil in a large saucepan over a medium high heat. Tip in the softened onions, bicarbonate of soda, thyme sprigs and bay leaves. Season with plenty of salt and pepper and fry for 15 minutes, stirring frequently, until dark golden brown. Stir in the flour and slowly add the stock, then simmer for 5 minutes.

Meanwhile, preheat the grill (broiler) to medium.

Spread the baguette slices out on a large, flat baking tray (pan), drizzle with the remaining garlic oil and grill (broil) for 1–3 minutes, turning halfway through, until golden brown. Remove from the grill and sprinkle over the cheese (don't worry if some falls on the tray – it will provide some crunchy bits). Turn the grill up to high and flash the cheese-topped toasts underneath until bubbling.

Meanwhile, ladle the soup into serving bowls. Use a spatula to pop a couple of slices of the cheesy toasts on top of each bowl of soup, and serve immediately. Retop with cheesy toasts as necessary.

Make ahead

Chop up the onions in advance and keep in the refrigerator for 1–2 days, or you can make the whole lot 2 days before you want to eat it, grilled cheese aside.

The shortcut

A few short minutes in the microwave reduces the overall cooking time of the soup and gets you to the good stuff faster, while the pinch of bicarb (baking soda) speeds up the browning and softening of the onions.

My minestrone

Serves	4
Prep	15 minutes
Cook	15 minutes

This is one of my go-to recipes and we eat it regularly, dressed up in myriad different ways – my favourite is with loads of olive oil, Parmesan and garlic-rubbed toasts. My family adore it and slurp lovingly.

I grate the vegetables directly into the pan to save time on chopping. Grating also means the veggies start cooking as soon as they hit the pan, not to mention cooking evenly at the same time. Since there is more surface area for flavour to develop, you start packing those sweet caramelised flavours into your soup immediately – so important when you need to harness all the flavour available in a short period of time.

I use orzo pasta, which are little grains of rice-shaped pasta that cook in a matter of minutes and release their starch to give the soup a satisfying body. You can use whatever pasta you have – just make it small. Broken-up spaghetti works a treat. I also stir in a generous amount of finely grated Parmesan at the end of the cooking time, which ensures that the all-important umami flavour is stirred throughout the soup while also transforming it into an unctuous bowl of goodness, packed full of vegetables and flavour.

1 tablespoon extra virgin olive oil, plus extra for drizzling
100 g (3½ oz/⅔ cup) smoked bacon lardons or pancetta cubes
2 carrots
1 onion, peeled
1 celery stalk
2 garlic cloves, peeled
2 fresh or dried bay leaves
½ teaspoon dried oregano
400 g (14 oz) tin good-quality chopped tomatoes
1 tablespoon red or white wine vinegar or cider vinegar
100 g (3½ oz) kale, chopped
75 g (2½ oz/⅓ cup) orzo pasta or small soup pasta
75 g (2½ oz/¾ cup) Parmesan or Cheddar, finely grated
sea salt and freshly ground black pepper

Heat the olive oil and the bacon lardons together in a large saucepan over a medium heat. Holding a box grater directly over the top of the pan, use the coarse side to grate in the carrots, onion and celery, then flip the grater around and finely grate in the garlic. Increase the heat to high and cook for 2–3 minutes, stirring frequently until the veg is soft.

Throw in the bay leaves, oregano and tinned tomatoes. Use the tomato tin to measure out 2½ tinfuls of water and add to the soup along with the vinegar. Stir in the kale and orzo, pushing them down with a spatula to submerge them in the liquid. Bring to a simmer, then partially cover and cook for 10 minutes, stirring from time to time.

Remove the pan from the heat, quickly add a quarter of the grated Parmesan and stir into the soup until melted – the soup should turn a creamy red colour and thicken slightly. Season well with salt and pepper and leave to stand for a few minutes. Ladle into bowls and serve drizzled with olive oil and plenty of the remaining Parmesan.

Make ahead

You can cook this up to the point of stirring in the cheese and keep in the refrigerator for 2–3 days or freeze for up to 3 months.

The shortcut

Grating instead of dicing will save a good 30 minutes, depending on how good or bad your knife skills are. Stirring in Parmesan thickens and adds a long-cooked mouthfeel without the time deficit.

Soups and salads

Asian-style chicken noodle soup

Serves 4
Prep 10 minutes
Cook 30 minutes

This is a deeply comforting soup that will fill your belly while nourishing you. It's a super easy one-pot soup that works well with most vegetables. Use the best quality chicken thighs you can afford as these are the base for the broth, and the meat is shredded up and eaten in the soup.

1–2 tablespoons sesame oil
6 skin-on, bone-in chicken thighs
6 spring onions (scallions), green and white parts separated and finely chopped
5 cm (2 in) piece of fresh root ginger, peeled and cut into matchsticks
4 garlic cloves, sliced
800 ml (27 fl oz/3¼ cups) cold water
2 tablespoons light soy sauce
2 tablespoons Chinese cooking wine or rice wine vinegar
¼ teaspoon caster (superfine) sugar
250 g (9 oz) dried fine egg noodles
4 pak choi (bok choi), halved lengthways
fermented black bean and chilli sauce or your favourite chilli sauce or chilli oil, to serve

Heat a drizzle of the sesame oil in a large saucepan over a medium heat. Add the chicken thighs, skin-side down, and leave to cook undisturbed for 3–5 minutes, or until the skin is golden brown. Flip over and cook for a further 3 minutes.

Push the chicken to one side and add a little more sesame oil to the pan, then add the white parts of the spring onions, along with the ginger and garlic. Fry for 2 minutes then pour in the cold water, soy sauce and Chinese cooking wine, along with any remaining sesame oil. Bring to the boil, then reduce the heat and simmer for 15 minutes. Taste for seasoning, adding more soy, rice wine or sesame oil as you feel necessary.

Use a slotted spoon to remove the chicken thighs from the soup. Discard the skin (if you don't like it) and the bones, then use a couple of forks to pull the meat apart.

Add the noodles to the soup and cook for 2 minutes, then add the pak choi and cook for a further 3 minutes until tender. Stir the shredded chicken back into the soup, then ladle into 4 serving bowls. Serve topped with the spring onion greens and a drizzle of chilli oil.

Make ahead

Make the soup base up to 3 days in advance, or cook and freeze the broth and chicken. Pre-cook your noodles and add to the soup with the greens.

The shortcut

This one-pot method means you waste no time in making a broth to then make a soup – it all works magically in one step.

Pork ramen

Serves	2
Prep	10 minutes
Cook	40 minutes

A good ramen, for me, is all about the broth – unctuous, rejuvenating and always satisfying. As we all know, a great broth takes a long time to make – developing depth of flavour is no easy feat. My method is far from authentic, but the result is a really tasty base for your ramen that is perfect when a packet of instant noodles won't do.

I use pork belly slices here (they're much easier to work with and cook much quicker than a whole piece of pork belly), along with a scattering of crushed-up, salty, sweet, umami-bomb pork scratchings/carnitas.

If you can't find ponzu, use 1 tablespoon of maple syrup mixed with 1 tablespoon of lemon juice.

2 eggs, at room temperature
4 slices of pork belly, cut into
    2 cm (¾ in) pieces
2 pork sausages, skins removed
2 anchovy fillets, finely chopped
4 spring onions (scallions),
    white and green parts
    separated and chopped
2 garlic cloves, chopped
2.5 cm (1 in) piece of fresh root
    ginger, sliced
1½ tablespoons miso paste
1½ tablespoons soy sauce
1 tablespoon ponzu
    (find it in the Asian food aisle)
1 litre (34 fl oz/4 cups) good-
    quality chicken or pork stock
300 g (10 oz) ready to eat udon
    noodles
1 large carrot, peeled with
    a julienne peeler or cut
    into matchsticks

To serve

60 g (2 oz) pork scratchings,
    lightly crushed
micro herbs (optional)
pinch of chilli (hot pepper) flakes
    (optional)
Japanese pickles

Cook the eggs in a pan of boiling water for 6 minutes, then drain and let cool. Peel the cooled eggs, then set aside.

Meanwhile, preheat the oven to 160°C/140°CFan/320°F/Gas 3.

Heat a large, deep frying pan (skillet) over a medium-high heat. Add the pork belly pieces and fry for 5 minutes, to render out some of the fat and colour lightly. Transfer to a baking tray (pan) and cook in the oven for 15 minutes.

Meanwhile, add the sausage meat to the same frying pan, along with the anchovies, and fry for 5 minutes, breaking the meat up with a wooden spoon until it resembles minced (ground) meat and is golden. Add the whites of the spring onions along with the garlic and ginger and fry for 2 minutes, stirring frequently until fragrant and softening.

Add the miso, soy and ponzu to the pan, then slowly add the stock, scraping the bottom of the pan to remove any pieces that have stuck. Bring to a gentle simmer and cook for 10 minutes. At this point you can strain the broth through a sieve for a clear broth, or just remove and discard the ginger.

Remove the pork belly from the oven and use a slotted spoon to lift the pork out of the tray and set aside. Pour away any fat, then scrape any sediment from the baking tray into the broth.

Add the noodles to the broth and heat through. Taste for seasoning, adding more soy and ponzu as necessary. Divide the noodles between 4 serving bowls, spoon over the broth and top with the pork belly, the spring onion greens, carrot slices, a handful of scratchings, some herbs and a sprinkling of chilli flakes, if using. Slice the cooked eggs in half and place one on top of each bowl. Serve immediately with some Japanese pickles.

Make ahead

You can make the broth ahead and keep in an airtight container for 5 days in the refrigerator, or you can put it into the freezer for at least 1 month.

The shortcut

The hack here is using some pork sausages fried up with aromatics and anchovy fillets for fat and funk – the fat in the sausages not only provides a deep porky flavour, but also gives the soup a viscosity that's deeply satisfying.

Soups and salads

Chicken and avocado Caesar salad

Serves 4
Prep 10 minutes
Cook 25 minutes

I feel so fortunate that Caesar salad exists, and chicken and avocado Caesar, well ... it is simply a bowl of all of my favourite things: anchovies, crunchy bread, roast chicken, avocado and, yes, lettuce!

Not all Caesar salads are created equal, and I like to think that this is up there with the best of them. I use a rotisserie chicken for ease, but also because they are always deliciously juicy, and that seasoned skin is just so good. Don't throw away any of the juices that gather in the container – here, they're poured over the bread before it's crisped up and the skin itself is roasted to crisp shards to be scattered over the salad before serving.

Making a Caesar dressing can seem tricky, but my version is easy: using a couple of tablespoons of good mayonnaise emulsifies the dressing and makes sure it clings to the salad ingredients. I also roast the lemon to make it super juicy and intensify the flavour. Making the dressing in a bowl big enough to fit all of the ingredients reduces the washing up and ensures you use every scrap of that delicious dressing.

1 oven-ready pre-cooked
    ciabatta loaf, torn into
    bite-size pieces
1 lemon, halved
olive oil, for drizzling
1 cooked rotisserie chicken
2 cos (romaine) lettuces,
    chopped into lengths
1 large ripe avocado, halved
    and stoned
sea salt and freshly ground
    black pepper

For the dressing

6 anchovy fillets in oil, drained
    and finely chopped
3 garlic cloves, chopped
4 tablespoons mayonnaise
50 g (2 oz) Parmesan cheese,
    finely grated
juice from 1 roasted lemon
    (see above)
1–2 tablespoons water
sea salt and freshly ground
    black pepper

Preheat the oven to 200°C/180°C Fan/400°F/Gas 6.

Put the ciabatta pieces on a baking tray (pan) with the lemon halves. Drizzle with olive oil and pour over any juices from the rotisserie chicken, then season with salt and pepper. Cook in the oven for 20 minutes, stirring the croutons and removing the lemon after 10 minutes.

Remove the meat from the chicken and tear it into chunks, setting the skin to one side (discard the bones). Lay the chicken skin on top of the croutons and return to the oven for a final 5 minutes to crisp up.

To make the dressing, put the anchovies and garlic on a board and use the back of a knife to crush them together into a paste. Scrape the paste into a large mixing bowl and add the mayonnaise, Parmesan, the juice from the roasted lemon halves and 1 tablespoon of the water. Stir to combine, adding more water if needed, until the dressing coats the back of a spoon. Taste for seasoning.

Add the lettuce, chicken meat and half of the croutons to the bowl with the dressing and toss to coat. Divide between serving plates and finish with the remaining croutons, scoops of avocado and the crispy chicken skin. Serve immediately, with an extra drizzle of olive oil if you like.

Make ahead

You can shred the chicken, cover and chill for up to 2 days. Make the dressing up to a week in advance and chill, then assemble the salad when ready to serve.

The shortcut

Using rotisserie chicken and doing minimal prep are both high-impact shortcuts. Restaurant-style Caesar salad made effortless.

Soups and salads

Niçoise salad

Serves	4
Prep	10 minutes
Cook	15 minutes

Nothing says summer like a Niçoise salad. I don't like to confine it just to summer, though, so I roll out this salad all year round. When something is this easy to prepare, why wouldn't you have it on repeat? Packed up for lunch, stuffed inside a baguette, eaten alongside a warming bowl of soup in the winter months, and then, it's summer again, the tomatoes are ripe and ready, and you have just what it takes to whip up a Niçoise right in front of your sun-kissed eyes (erm, wishful thinking!).

This is a super-versatile salad and you can mix and match the ingredients to suit what is in season, if you like. If the tomatoes aren't good, leave them out and use a handful of sundried tomatoes. If your green beans are looking limp, stir in some tinned cannellini beans in their place. And if fresh tuna is on offer, throw it on the griddle and slice it up to take this salad to very special status.

For maximum flavour, let your potatoes and green beans cool in the vinaigrette.

12 baby potatoes
4 large eggs
100 g (3½ oz) green beans
2 baby gem (bibb) lettuces,
    broken into separate leaves
2 red (bell) peppers from a jar,
    drained and torn into strips
200 g (7 oz) vine-ripened cherry
    tomatoes, chopped
100 g (3½ oz) mixed olives
    (I love stuffed green, Kalamata
    or Niçoise), torn if large
2 x 200g tins tuna in oil, drained
crusty bread, to serve

For the dressing

6 anchovy fillets, finely chopped
2 tablespoons baby capers
2 garlic cloves, grated
1 tablespoon Dijon mustard
2 tablespoons red wine vinegar
4 tablespoons olive oil, plus
    extra for drizzling
sea salt and freshly ground
    black pepper
large handful of flat-leaf parsley,
    roughly chopped

First, make the dressing in the same large bowl that you will use to serve up the salad. Mix together the anchovies, capers, garlic, mustard, vinegar, olive oil and plenty of seasoning. Stir in most of the parsley, then set aside.

Bring a large saucepan of salted water to the boil. Add the potatoes and eggs and cook for 6 minutes, then add the green beans and cook for a further 4 minutes. Drain, setting the eggs to one side, then tip the potatoes and beans into the bowl with the dressing and toss to coat. Cool the eggs under running cold water, then drain again. Peel and halve each egg, then set aside.

Add the lettuce, red peppers and tomatoes to the potatoes and beans, and gently toss to combine. Scatter over the olives and flake over the tuna. Top with the egg halves and the remaining parsley, then serve immediately with a drizzle of olive oil and some crusty bread.

Make ahead

Everything for this recipe can be done in advance and combined just before serving, making it a perfect entertaining dish or ideal to pack up for work lunches throughout the week.

The shortcut

By cooking the potatoes, eggs and green beans in just the one pan and making the dressing directly in the serving bowl, you save a good 15 minutes on washing up alone.

Soups and salads

Marinated kale and brown rice salad (green bowls)

Serves 2
Prep 15 minutes
Cook 10 minutes

Okay, so you bought a big bag of kale in an attempt at health and now you need to use it up ... this is the perfect recipe for you. It's kale three ways: marinated as the base of your salad, whizzed up into a garlicky pesto and crisped up to a salty, crunchy topping. The ultimate green bowl.

Adding miso to the pesto here is just genius as you get a great umami hit without needing the more traditional Parmesan. And I promise if you invest in a jar of nutritional yeast, it will become your new BF in the kitchen. I sprinkle it on everything from savoury porridge to popcorn.

200 g (7 oz) curly kale, tough stalks removed
250 g (9 oz) packet microwave wholegrain brown rice
1 large avocado, halved and stoned
1 tablespoon pickled ginger, shredded
1 tablespoon toasted sesame seeds

For the marinated kale
1 tablespoon light-flavoured oil
½ teaspoon sesame oil
1 tablespoon maple syrup
juice of ½ lemon
sea salt and freshly ground black pepper

For the kale chips
1 tablespoon light-flavoured oil
1 teaspoon nutritional yeast
¼ teaspoon dried chilli (hot pepper) flakes
½ teaspoon salt

For the kale pesto
2 tablespoons light-flavoured oil
½ teaspoon sesame oil
½ garlic clove, grated
1½ tablespoons white miso paste
large handful of coriander (cilantro), roughly chopped

First, make your marinated kale. In a large bowl, mix a third of the kale with the light-flavoured oil, sesame oil, maple syrup and lemon juice. Season really well, then massage the kale for about 3 minutes – this will start to break down the leaves, tenderising them. Set aside.

Preheat the grill (broiler) to high.

To make the kale chips, mix another third of the kale in a large bowl with the light-flavoured oil, nutritional yeast, chilli flakes and salt. Lay in a single layer on a baking sheet and grill (broil) for 3–4 minutes, or until the kale is starting to char at the edges. Turn the kale over and grill for a further 1 minute, then remove from the grill and set aside.

Next, make the kale pesto. Put the remaining third of the kale into a microwave-safe bowl, add 1 teaspoon of water, cover and cook on high in the microwave for 2 minutes. Remove from the microwave and scrape into the bowl of a food processor. Add the light-flavoured oil and sesame oil, grate in the garlic, then add the miso paste, coriander stems and most of the leaves. Process to a paste, then transfer the pesto to a mixing bowl.

Cook the brown rice according to the packet instructions, tip into the kale pesto and stir to coat.

Divide the pesto-coated rice between 2 serving bowls. Top each bowl with a scoop of the marinated kale, along with any resting juices, a handful of kale chips, an avocado half, a little shredded pickled ginger, a generous sprinkling of sesame seeds and the remaining coriander leaves.

Make ahead

Make all of the components of this salad up to a week in advance. Store the kale chips in an airtight container, the marinated kale in the fridge and the pesto in a jar under a layer of light-flavoured oil.

The shortcut

I use pre-cooked brown rice because I can be impatient ... and brown rice takes some time to cook. If you are more patient than me, then cook away, but add on an extra 30–40 minutes to your prep time.

Smoky aubergine dip (and a pull-together mezze feast)

Serves	2–4
Prep	15 minutes
Cook	20 minutes

Got an impromptu gathering of friends at your place and don't know what to serve? Make a mezze. When I say 'make', what I mean is: make one knock-out dish of my smoky aubergine (eggplant) dip and cheat the rest. I'm going to show you how to make something store-bought look and taste cookbook-worthy with a few tricks of the trade.

It may seem as though the same ingredients are used a lot in these mezze dishes, but they achieve such different flavours when used in different combinations.

2 aubergines (eggplants),
  pricked all over with a fork
200 g (7 oz/¾ cup) Greek yoghurt
3 tablespoons tahini, plus extra
  for drizzling
½ garlic clove, grated
1 lemon, zested and halved
  for squeezing
olive oil, for drizzling
400 g (14 oz) mixed olives
Turkish red pepper flakes,
  for sprinkling
250 g (9 oz) tub store-bought
  hummus
paprika, for sprinkling
4 Lebanese cucumbers,
  roughly chopped
8 ripe tomatoes, roughly chopped
250 g (9 oz) halloumi, sliced
honey, for drizzling
za'atar, for sprinkling (optional)
12 store-bought falafel,
  cooked according to packet
  instructions and kept warm
handful of pomegranate seeds
small bunch of flat-leaf parsley
  leaves, roughly chopped
sea salt and freshly ground
  black pepper
flatbreads, pittas or naan
  breads, to serve

Heat a grill (broiler) or a large gas stove burner to high. Put the aubergines directly over the flame and cook for 10 minutes, turning frequently, until charred all over and soft. Transfer to a large sealable plastic bag, seal and leave to cool.

Halve the cooled aubergines lengthways and use a spoon to scrape out the flesh. Transfer it to a serving bowl, then add the yoghurt, 2 tablespoons of the tahini, the grated garlic and a good squeeze of the lemon juice and mash together. Season well and stir to combine, then taste and add more of the smoky liquid that will have collected in the plastic bag, if you like. Drizzle with olive oil.

Put the olives in a bowl, top with the lemon zest, drizzle with olive oil and sprinkle with pepper flakes. Set aside.

Empty the hummus into a serving dish and stir in a squeeze of lemon juice and 1 tablespoon of the tahini. Use the back of a spoon to create a well in the middle and fill it with a drizzle of olive oil. Sprinkle with paprika and set aside.

Put the cucumbers and tomatoes on a serving dish and sprinkle with salt and pepper flakes. Set aside.

Heat a large non-stick frying pan (skillet) over a high heat. Cook the halloumi slices for 1–2 minutes on each side or until golden on the outside and soft in the middle. Remove to a serving plate, then drizzle with honey and sprinkle with za'atar.

Put the hot falafel on a serving platter, drizzle with some more tahini, and sprinkle over the pomegranate seeds and some chopped parsley.

Warm the flatbreads for a few minutes in the hot oven, then bring to the table with all the mezze dishes and some olive oil for drizzling. Scatter the remaining parsley over the spread, so you can grab them and eat them with the mezze.

Make ahead

Make the dip up to 3 days in advance and chill until required.

The shortcut

Making one dish but presenting six ... that's a whole day's worth of cooking saved.

Soups and salads

Pork

&

chicken

The easiest roast chicken dinner

Serves 4
Prep 15 minutes, plus
30 minutes standing
Cook 1 hour, plus
10 minutes standing

This is such an easy way to roast a chicken. The garlic salt that is rubbed on at the start really gets into the meat, acting as both seasoning and brine, keeping your bird ultra-juicy – this is a little trick I picked up from my local Portuguese restaurant. The oven should be really hot when you put your chicken in to cook, so that the bird starts to cook instantly, which helps reduce the overall cooking time. Resting the chicken is essential and will ensure your bird is really juicy.

The chicken is cooked on top of the veg. The reason for this is two-fold: one, the veg is cooked in and covered with delicious chicken juices, and two, sitting the chicken on top of the veg rather than nestling it into the veg allows the heat to circulate all around the bird, ensuring an even and quick roast. I love the combination of veg specified – but honestly, just cook what you love. If that's just potatoes, then be my guest.

1 fat garlic clove, grated
1.3 kg (3 lb) whole chicken
8 sprigs of thyme or rosemary
½ lemon or tangerine
2 onions, cut into wedges
16 baby new potatoes, halved
1 small or ½ large swede
(rutabaga), peeled and
cut into 2.5 cm (1 in) dice
½ red cabbage, cut into
wedges through the root
drizzle of olive oil
4 large carrots, quartered
lengthways
2 tablespoons butter, softened
drizzle of olive oil
fine sea salt and freshly ground
black pepper

Mix 1 tablespoon of salt with the garlic to form a grainy paste, then rub the chicken inside and out with the paste. Stuff half of the thyme sprigs and the lemon half into the bird's cavity, then let the chicken stand for 30 minutes at room temperature.

Meanwhile, preheat the oven to 220°C/200°C Fan/430°F/Gas 8.

Take a large baking tray (pan), about 3 cm (1¼ in) deep, which should be deep enough to contain the veg but not so deep that it covers the sides of the chicken. Arrange the veg over the bottom of the tray. Rub the softened butter over the breast of the chicken and sit it on top of the vegetables. Drizzle the oil over the veg, scatter with the remaining thyme and season with salt and pepper.

Roast in the hot oven for 30 minutes. After 30 minutes, move the veg under the chicken about a bit, reduce the oven temperature to 200°C/180°C Fan/400°F/Gas 6 and return the tray to the oven to roast for another 30 minutes.

Lift the chicken off the veg, place it on a serving dish and allow to rest in a warm spot for at least 10 minutes. Give the veg another stir and return to the oven to keep warm.

Carve the chicken and serve with the vegetables and any pan juices.

Make ahead

You can prep the veg and keep it in the refrigerator for 2 days.

The shortcut

Cooking at a higher temperature with a shorter cooking time means that roast chicken doesn't have to be relegated to the weekends. You can even have a roast chicken on a miserable Monday – imagine!

Chicken, leek and mushroom pot pie

Serves 4–6
Prep 10 minutes
Cook 35 minutes

Chicken pie is so warming and comforting. If somebody made me a pie, I would really feel as though they'd gone all-out to make me feel the love. That's how I want to make people feel when I cook for them … but I don't always want to go all-out in my pursuit of making a pie. Sometimes, I want to get a delicious pie on the table quickly, while still delivering warm hugs and love.

I use pre-cooked chicken thighs or a rotisserie chicken in my pies, as they're cooked to perfection and seasoned well, and the base of my sauce is double (heavy) cream. I also cook the leek and mushrooms in the microwave – who'd have thought that mushrooms could taste so good after a few minutes in the microwave?

If you love making pastry, be my guest, but I use store-bought puff pastry. It delivers everything I want from a puff-pastry pie crust, especially if you use the all-butter kind – rich, flaky layers and a crisp golden top to your pie.

1 large leek, sliced
200 g (7 oz) chestnut (cremini) mushrooms, sliced
2 garlic cloves, grated
2 tablespoons butter
4 sprigs of thyme
1 tablespoon Dijon mustard
250 ml (8½ fl oz/1 cup) double (heavy) cream
½ chicken stock cube
60 ml (2 fl oz/ very scant ½ cup) boiling water
500 g (1 lb 2 oz) pre-cooked skinless, boneless chicken thighs or breasts, roughly chopped
375 g (13 oz) pack all-butter puff pastry
1 egg yolk, beaten
sea salt and freshly ground black pepper

Preheat the oven to 200°C/180°C Fan/400°F/Gas 6.

Put the leeks, mushrooms and garlic in a large, microwave-safe bowl, season with salt and pepper and dot over the butter. Cover tightly and cook in the microwave for 4 minutes, stirring halfway through.

Add the thyme, mustard and double cream to the bowl. Place the stock cube in a jug and pour over the boiling water. Once the stock cube has dissolved, stir the stock into the mushroom and leek mixture. Add the chicken, then scrape the whole lot into a 20 x 28 cm (8 x 11 in) pie dish.

Roll out the puff pastry so that it is just bigger than the pie dish. Cover the dish with the puff pastry lid, pushing it up to the edges of the pot. Trim off any overhanging pastry, score a couple of steam holes through the top and glaze with the beaten egg yolk. Bake for 30 minutes, or until the pastry is golden and puffed up.

Make ahead

The whole pie can be prepped ahead and kept in the refrigerator unbaked for 2 days, or frozen for up to 2 months, then thawed and cooked.

The shortcut

A roast chicken pie without roasting a chicken, perfectly tender leeks and mushrooms with no frying pan (skillet), and a rich, creamy sauce without the whisking? A weekend project turns into a weeknight dinner here.

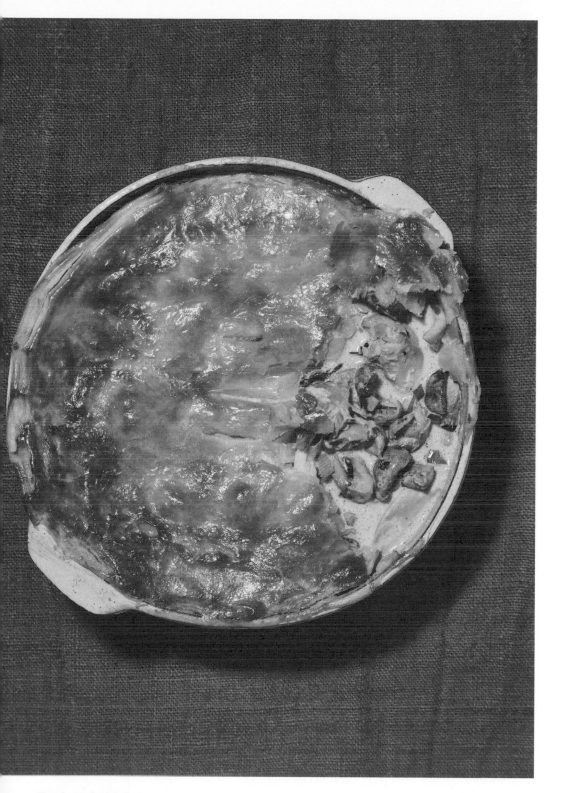

Pork and chicken

My chicken biryani

Serves	4
Prep	10 minutes
Cook	35 minutes

Traditional biryanis can take a lot of time to prepare, from marinating the meat to soaking and part-cooking the rice, before assembling the dish to be steamed while enclosed in a dough-sealed pot. My version is a whole lot simpler, without sacrificing the flavours of this celebratory dish.

To speed things up and ensure you get beautiful individual grains of rice, pre-soak your basmati rice in warm water. This swells the rice and reduces the cooking time. I use an all-in-one cooking method, removing the need to pre-cook the rice. Cutting the chicken into bite-size chunks means it cooks quickly and the flavour of the spices can be absorbed all over.

Many biryani recipes call for crispy fried onions. There is no way I will ever pass up a fried onion, but these are tricky to get just right. Fear not: crispy onions (or shallots) are easy to find in the World Food aisle of stores or in Asian supermarkets – so please, buy them pre-made.

400 g (14 oz/2 cups) basmati rice
2 tablespoons butter
1 tablespoon light-flavoured oil
1 onion, thinly sliced
1 green finger chilli, chopped
6 cardamom pods, bashed
5 cm (2 in) piece of cinnamon
  stick, broken in half
5 cm (2 in) piece of fresh root
  ginger, grated
4 garlic cloves, grated
2 teaspoons garam masala
3 teaspoons ground cumin
½ teaspoon turmeric
1 teaspoon chilli powder
6 skinless, boneless chicken
  thighs, cut into bite-size pieces
50 g (2 oz/¾ cup) crispy
  fried onions
750–850 ml (25–28 fl oz/
  3–3½ cups) boiling water
large handful of coriander
  (cilantro), chopped
handful of toasted flaked
  (slivered) almonds
fine sea salt and freshly ground
  black pepper
natural yoghurt, to serve
  (optional)

Soak the rice in a large bowl of warm water for 15 minutes, then drain and rinse under cold running water until the water runs clear. Put the kettle on to boil.

Meanwhile, heat the butter and oil in a deep frying pan (skillet) or a flameproof casserole dish (Dutch oven) set over a medium heat. Fry the onion, chilli, cardamom pods and cinnamon stick for 5 minutes, stirring frequently.

Meanwhile, in a large bowl, mix the grated ginger and garlic with the dried spices, ½ teaspoon salt and a generous grinding of black pepper. Add the chicken and massage the spice mix into the meat.

Add the chicken to the pan and fry for 5 minutes until the chicken has changed colour and the spices are fragrant. Stir in half of the crispy fried onions and season really well.

Scatter the rice over the chicken in an even layer, then pour over the boiling water and add ½ teaspoon salt. The rice should be just submerged under the water. Agitate the rice with a spoon but don't stir. Bring to the boil and cook for 6 minutes. Cover with foil and a tight-fitting lid to seal in the steam, then turn off the heat and leave to stand, undisturbed, for 10 minutes.

Remove the lid and foil and sprinkle with the remaining fried onions, coriander leaves and flaked almonds. Serve immediately with yoghurt on the side if you like.

Make ahead

You can keep the marinated chicken in the refrigerator for 24 hours before cooking, and rinse the rice a day ahead, too.

The shortcut

Biryani can take hours to prepare – this method, with pre-soaked rice and store-bought onions, will have it on the table in under an hour.

Pork and chicken

A really good chicken curry

Serves 4, with leftovers
Prep 15 minutes
Cook 20 minutes

My favourite chicken curry, like so many, is a tikka masala. The chicken is cooked in a tandoor or clay oven before being stirred through a creamy base sauce. I have adapted this method for my kitchen. Grilling (broiling) the chicken packs in extra flavour as the marinade caramelises and the meat gets nicely charred, plus cooking it over a high heat reduces the overall cooking time. The chicken can be grilled in advance, and the sauce can be made in advance, too, meaning all you need to do is reheat the meat in the curry sauce when you're ready to serve.

I use coconut milk in my chicken curry because it's rich and creamy and packed full of flavour – so important when you're making a quick curry. Curry pastes are brilliant to have in the refrigerator, as they're full of spices in the right combinations and get you to a really good curry in … well … a hurry!

4 garlic cloves, grated
8 cm (3½ in) piece of fresh root ginger, grated
3 green chillies, roughly chopped, plus extra to serve
large handful of coriander (cilantro), leaves and stems separated and finely chopped
4 tablespoons tikka masala paste
8 skinless, boneless chicken thighs, quartered
light-flavoured oil, for frying
1 onion, chopped
1 tablespoon garam masala or curry powder
400 g (14 oz) tin chopped tomatoes
½ x 400 ml (14 fl oz) tin coconut milk
sea salt and freshly ground black pepper

To serve

boiled rice, popadoms and chutney, to serve

Preheat the grill (broiler) to high.

Mix half of the garlic, ginger, green chillies and coriander stalks in a large bowl and stir through half of the tikka masala paste. Add the chopped chicken and use your hands to rub the paste into the chicken.

Lay the chicken in a single layer on a lightly greased baking tray (pan) and grill (broil) for 5 minutes, turning halfway, or until the chicken is cooked through and charred in places.

Meanwhile, set a large non-stick frying pan (skillet) over a medium–high heat, add a generous drizzle of oil and fry the onion for 5 minutes, or until starting to soften. Tip in the remaining garlic, ginger and green chillies, along with the remaining tikka masala paste, and fry for 1 minute. Add the garam masala, chopped tomatoes and coconut milk, bring to the boil and bubble for 5 minutes. Reduce the heat, then add the cooked chicken and any pan juices to the curry sauce. Stir to combine and cook for a few minutes, then taste for seasoning.

Scatter over the remaining coriander leaves and serve with boiled rice, extra chillies, popadoms and chutney, if you like.

Make ahead

The sauce can be made in advance, and the chicken can be cooked under the grill (broiler), then cooled, and stored in the refrigerator for 24 hours. Just drop it into the reheated curry sauce when ready to serve.

The shortcut

Again, a high cooking temperature and flavour-packed ingredients are your friends here – despite the quick cooking time, you're left with an unctuous sauce that tastes as though it's been simmering for hours.

Pork and chicken

Smoky paprika chicken with warm cannellini beans

Serves 2
Prep 10 minutes, plus standing
Cook 50 minutes

Mayonnaise is used in this recipe as the base of a marinade for the chicken and also as the accompaniment to the dish. The great thing about using mayo is that it stays in place and doesn't slip off as the chicken cooks and gets hot; it also keeps the chicken from drying out, as it forms a protective layer on the outside.

Try adding different ingredients to the mayo to flavour the chicken – here I have used smoked paprika and garlic, a twist on classic Spanish flavours.

Add vine tomatoes to the hot tray at the end of cooking to soften them, squishing a few to make a warm dressing for the cannellini beans. This really is a super-easy, one-pan meal that I am sure will become a family favourite.

6 tablespoons mayonnaise
3 teaspoons smoked paprika
2 garlic cloves, grated
2 chicken leg portions, scored 2–3 times
200 g (7 oz) cherry vine tomatoes, cut into small bunches
1 tablespoon sherry vinegar
400 g (14 oz) tin cannellini beans, drained
large handful of flat-leaf parsley, roughly chopped
sea salt and freshly ground black pepper

In a large bowl, mix together the mayonnaise, smoked paprika and grated garlic, then remove two thirds to a small bowl and set aside.

Spread the remaining mayo over the chicken legs, rubbing it into the scores. Lay the chicken on a baking tray (pan) and leave to marinate for 30 minutes.

Meanwhile, preheat the oven to 220°C/200°C Fan/430°F/Gas 8.

Cook the chicken in the hot oven for 40 minutes, then remove it from the oven and add the tomatoes to the tray. Return to the oven for a further 10 minutes, or until the chicken is cooked through and golden. Transfer the chicken to a plate to rest.

Squash a couple of the tomatoes, add the vinegar and scrape up any juices at the bottom of the tray to make a dressing. Tip the cannellini beans into the tray, stirring to coat them with the warm dressing and any resting juices from the chicken. Taste for seasoning.

Spoon the dressed beans out into a serving dish, top with the chicken and scatter with the parsley. Serve immediately, with the reserved smoky paprika mayonnaise on the side.

Make ahead

Prep the marinade and rub over the chicken legs 2 days in advance and store in an airtight container.

The shortcut

Squashing a couple of cooked ripe tomatoes in the tray to make a dressing for the beans not only saves on washing up, but instantly harnesses all those pan juices. Scoring the chicken legs ensures the marinade goes deep into the meat and speeds up the cooking time.

Pork and chicken

Fried chicken

Serves	4
Prep	5 minutes, plus 30 minutes standing
Cook	40 minutes

The shortest route to fried chicken heaven is right here. Believe me, I ate my way around many variations of this dish, and I wound up here. This recipe is so simple and really delivers.

Seasoning the chicken before you dip it in the coating acts like a brine; as the chicken sits, the seasoning penetrates the meat, meaning you get great flavour deep into the chicken, not just in the coating. The buttermilk-and-milk combo allows the coating to stick and acts as a tenderiser for the meat, while using a combination of flours delivers a super-crunchy coating.

You will need a pan thermometer. Cooking your chicken at the right temperature will help to seal the crust as soon as it hits the hot fat, which in turn keeps those juices inside the chicken. It also prevents the crust from becoming soggy.

Before you start dipping your chicken, fill your kitchen sink with hot soapy water and grab a clean dish towel so you can wash and dry your hands if you need to. Also, line a large tray with paper towels with a wire rack on top to drain your chicken after frying.

8 skin-on, bone-in chicken thighs
75 g (2½ oz/scant ⅔ cup) cornflour (cornstarch)
150 g (5 oz/1¼ cups) plain (all-purpose) flour
150 ml (5 fl oz/scant ⅔ cup) buttermilk
100 ml (3½ fl oz/scant ½ cup) whole (full-fat) milk
rapeseed (canola) oil, for deep-frying
fine sea salt and freshly ground black pepper

About 30 minutes before you want to cook, take the chicken out of the refrigerator and lay it on a tray. Season well on both sides, using about 1½ teaspoons salt and 1 teaspoon black pepper.

Mix together the cornflour and plain flour on a plate with a good pinch of fine salt. Combine the buttermilk and milk in a bowl.

Preheat the oven to a low heat. Pour oil to a depth of 5 cm (2 in) depth in a high-sided, heavy-based pan and set it over a medium–high heat. Heat the oil to 160°C/320°F using a pan (sugar) thermometer to measure the temperature.

Take a piece of chicken, dip it into the buttermilk, shake off any excess, then dip it into the flour, patting off any excess, then back into the buttermilk and finally back into the flour. Pat off any excess flour – the chicken will look very craggy.

Carefully lower the chicken into the hot oil using tongs and fry for 10 minutes, turning a couple of times, until golden and very crisp. Stay with the pan and regulate the heat to ensure the oil stays at the right temperature. You will have to cook the chicken in batches, usually 2 pieces at a time. Remove the fried chicken and drain on a wire rack set over a paper towel- lined tray. Keep the cooked chicken warm in the oven while you fry the rest. Serve with your choice of sides.

Make ahead

You can cook the whole lot 24 hours in advance and reheat to serve – great if you're havng guests over so you can clear all the (minimal) mess out of the way the day before.

The shortcut

No brining means no need to plan ahead – great fried chicken in 1 hour, instead of 24 hours.

Pork and chicken

Crispy sticky chicken wings

Serves 4 (or 2 with
a healthy appetite)
Prep 10 minutes
Cook 40 minutes

These chicken wings are oven-baked, but adding a pinch of bicarbonate of soda (baking soda) to the dry rub before they're cooked makes them super crispy – as if they've been deep-fried when really you're let the oven do all the hard work for you.

Make sure you put the wings into a cold oven – as it warms up, the fat from the chicken begins to render out, allowing the skin to crisp up once the oven is hot.

The sweet, spicy, sticky glaze is the stuff of dreams – how could it not be, when it's a combination of all the good things from your storecupboard? I like to toss the wings in a little of the glaze at the end of cooking and then serve the rest as a dipping sauce.

I don't like to give a serving number for wings because I know my own ability to scoff wings is remarkable, so if – like me – you have a very healthy appetite and appreciation for wings, then double or even treble the recipe.

1.5 kg (3 lbs 5 oz) chicken wings
½ teaspoon bicarbonate of soda
(baking soda)
1 teaspoon salt
1 teaspoon Chinese five spice
pinch of ground turmeric

For the sticky sauce

3 tablespoons soy sauce
3 tablespoons rice vinegar
3 tablespoons Sriracha chilli sauce
3 tablespoons soft light
brown sugar
2 tablespoons honey
4 cm (1½ in) piece of fresh root
ginger, finely grated
2 garlic cloves, grated
zest of 1 tangerine

To serve (optional)

toasted sesame seeds,
for sprinkling

Take the chicken wings out of the refrigerator about 20–30 minutes before you want to start cooking and pat them dry with paper towels. Place the wings in a single layer on a couple of large baking trays (pans).

In a small bowl, mix together the bicarbonate of soda, salt, Chinese five spice and turmeric. Scatter this all over the wings, pressing the mixture into the skin with your fingertips. Put the chicken into the cold oven and turn the heat to 220°C/200°C Fan/430°F/Gas 8. Cook for 30 minutes.

Meanwhile, make the sticky sauce. Put all the sauce ingredients into a small saucepan set over a medium heat. Bring to the boil and cook stirring frequently, until the sugar has dissolved, then bubble for a further 2 minutes. Remove from the heat and pour half of the sauce into a large mixing bowl and the other half into a dipping bowl.

Remove the cooked chicken wings from the oven and toss them with the sticky glaze in the mixing bowl. Transfer them back to the baking trays. Spoon any glaze left in the bowl over the wings and cook for a final 5 minutes.

Pile the sticky wings on to a serving plate and scatter over the sesame seeds, if using. Serve with the additional sauce for dipping.

Make ahead

You can make the glaze 4–5 days in advance and keep it chilled. Just remember to take it out of the refrigerator at the same time as the wings to come to room temperature.

The shortcut

No deep-fried facial, no grease disposal, no standing over a pot of boiling oil. My kind of shortcut.

Sausage ragù

Serves	4
Prep	10 minutes
Cook	20 minutes

This dish is perfect when you need something comforting and packed full of flavour, but you don't have time for a slow-cooked ragù – it's a super-quick, luxurious-tasting meal.

Use the best sausages you can find, because these will form the basis of your dish. I like Italian-style pork sausages, but feel free to use chicken sausages, too. The beauty of sausages is that they cook down quickly and there is plenty of surface area and fat to develop a rich flavour when it hits the hot pan.

This isn't a traditional ragù, as I don't use tomatoes or red wine in the sauce.

The pasta water makes the sauce silky as it emulsifies with the juices from the sausages and the cheese.

Give it a try – it will become a regular fixture on your weekly meal planner.

400 g (14 oz) dried pasta
  (penne or rigatoni work well)
2 tablespoons olive oil
6 good-quality pork sausages,
  skins removed
1 fennel bulb, thinly sliced,
  fronds reserved
1 onion, thinly sliced
1 teaspoon fennel seeds
½ teaspoon dried chilli
  (hot pepper) flakes
2 garlic cloves, chopped
1 chicken stock cube
2 tablespoons butter
sea salt and freshly ground
  black pepper
Parmesan or pecorino cheese,
  grated, to serve

Cook the pasta according to the packet instructions in a saucepan of boiling water.

Meanwhile, heat the oil in a large, shallow flameproof casserole dish (Dutch oven) set over a medium-high heat. Add the sausages and fry for 5 minutes, using a wooden spoon to break up the meat into small chunks as you go. Push the sausage meat to one side, add the fennel and onion, and fry for 3 minutes, stirring frequently. Mix the sausage meat back into the vegetables, then add the fennel seeds, chilli flakes and garlic, and fry for 1 minute.

Drain the cooked pasta, reserving the cooking water.

Crumble the stock cube into the ragù. Measure out 250 ml (8½ fl oz/1 cup) of the pasta cooking water and pour it into the dish, stirring to dissolve the stock cube. Cook for a further 10 minutes.

Remove the ragù from the heat, add the butter and shake the pan to melt it and thicken the sauce. Season to taste. Toss the pasta through the ragù and serve topped with the reserved fennel fronds and the grated Parmesan.

Make ahead

You could make the whole thing in advance, then reheat – just make sure you reduce the pasta cooking time by 1–2 minutes.

The shortcut

Sausages bring all the flavour with minimum effort – it's worth having a few ideas like this up your sleeve for those nights when you need comfort food, fast.

Pork and chicken

Brined pork chops with creamy rosemary white beans

Serves 2
Prep 10 minutes, plus 1 hour brining
Cook 20 minutes

Brining your chops ensures tender meat and flavour throughout. I flavour the brine with aromatic rosemary and a hint of chilli. Before you cook your chops, make sure the surface of the meat is really dry. I love serving these with creamy rosemary white beans. It's a quick and very easy alternative to a baked potato or mash – the beans heat through in a matter of minutes and the cream brings a luxurious touch, which makes this a perfect meal when you want to look as though you've made an effort when in reality you've done very little. Plus, you only use one pan.

3 sprigs of rosemary: 1 whole sprig; 2 finely chopped
3 garlic cloves: 1 whole clove; 2 grated
1 red chilli, halved lengthways
2 tablespoons fine sea salt
3 tablespoons boiling water
150 ml (5 fl oz/scant ⅔ cup) cold water
2 pork chops, pricked all over with a toothpick
1 tablespoon olive oil, plus a drizzle
1½ tablespoon butter
1 onion, finely chopped
200 ml (7 fl oz/scant 1 cup) double (heavy) cream
2 x 400 g (14 oz) tins butter (lima) beans, drained
50 g (2 oz) Cheddar cheese, grated
sea salt and freshly ground black pepper

Bash the whole rosemary sprig and whole garlic clove on a chopping board with the back of a knife to release some of their natural oils. Put them into a medium-sized oven dish along with the red chilli and salt. Pour over the boiling water and stir to dissolve the salt, then top up with the cold water. Submerge the pork chops in the brine and leave to stand for 1 hour, turning them every 15 minutes.

Remove the pork chops from the brine, shaking off any excess, and dry them as thoroughly as possible with kitchen towel.

Heat a drizzle of the oil in a large frying pan (skillet) with a heatproof handle set over a high heat. Add the chops and fry for 5 minutes, turning halfway through. At the halfway point, throw in the butter and baste the chops with the melted butter as they fry. Stand the chops up on their sides with the layer of fat touching the pan and cook for a further few minutes to crisp up. Remove from the pan and leave to rest.

Return the pan to the heat, add the olive oil and onion, and fry for 3 minutes. Then add the finely chopped rosemary leaves and grated garlic, and fry for 1 minute. Pour in the cream and bring to a simmer. Add the beans, roughly breaking up about a third of them with a wooden spoon. Season with plenty of pepper and a pinch of salt. Bubble for a further 5 minutes until the cream has thickened.

Meanwhile, preheat the grill (broiler) to high.

Sprinkle the cheese over the beans and flash the pan under the hot grill until the cheese is golden and bubbling. Serve immediately with the pork chops.

Make ahead

You can make the brine ahead and let your chops sit in the refrigerator for up to 6 hours. The butter (lima) beans can be made ahead and reheated for 10 minutes.

The shortcut

Creamy, cheesy beans instead of a dauphinoise has all the glamour, none of the prep. And one pan, once again, means the bare minimum of washing-up.

Pork and chicken

Spicy pork loin with rice noodles

Serves 4
Prep 10 minutes
Cook 6 minutes, plus
5 minutes resting

This recipe calls for just a few ingredients, minimal effort and not much cooking skill. It's the kind of recipe you will revisit on a busy week night when you want something super-tasty that looks great and is easy to prepare. I use sweet chilli sauce because it already packs the sweet spicy chilli flavours called for here.

Use thin-cut boneless pork loin steaks or boneless chops – these will cook in a matter of minutes. If you don't eat pork, steak would be a great alternative. I love using my griddle pan, but a barbecue would be great, or even a frying pan. Don't forget to take your chops out of the refrigerator 20–30 minutes in advance so they're not fridge-cold.

Rice noodles should be a pantry staple for the time-poor hungry cook, as they don't need to be boiled – just cover with boiling water and leave to stand. They are also brilliant flavour-carriers and their slightly chewy, yet comforting texture works brilliantly with the thinly sliced pork and spicy dressing.

200g (7 oz) instant vermicelli
  rice noodles
4 boneless pork loin chops
4 spring onions (scallions),
  chopped
½ cucumber, cut into matchsticks
  with a julienne peeler
2 carrots, cut into matchsticks
  with a julienne peeler
large handful of coriander
  (cilantro) leaves
large handful of mint leaves
handful of salted peanuts,
  roughly chopped
½ juicy lime, cut into wedges,
  to serve

For the spicy dressing
4 tablespoons sweet chilli sauce
2½ tablespoons soy sauce,
  or more as needed
1½ tablespoons fish sauce,
  to taste
juice of ½ juicy lime

First, make the dressing. Mix together the sweet chilli sauce, soy sauce, fish sauce and lime juice in a small bowl. Taste for seasoning and add a little more soy or fish sauce, as needed.

Meanwhile, fill the kettle and put it on to boil. Put the rice noodles in a large bowl and pour over enough boiling water to completely submerge the noodles. Leave to stand for 3 minutes. Drain and refresh under cold running water, then drain again. Toss the noodles with half of the dressing.

Heat a griddle pan over a high heat. Cook the chops for 2–3 minutes on each side (depending on their thickness). Transfer to a plate, spoon over a little of the dressing and leave to rest for 5 minutes.

Add the remaining ingredients (except the peanuts and lime wedges) to the noodles and toss to combine. Thinly slice the griddled pork and add to the noodles, along with any resting juices and the remaining dressing. Serve immediately, scattered with the peanuts and with the lime wedges on the side.

Make ahead

You can cook the noodles, refresh under cold water and drizzle with a little oil, then store, covered, in the refrigerator for up to 2 days. The pork can be cooked and chilled for up to 2 days and the dressing will happily sit in the refrigerator for up to 1 week.

The shortcut

A couple of store-bought ingredients really maximise the flavour here, along with a little bit of easy peeling with either a julienne peeler or a speed peeler, usually reserved for your potatoes.

Pork and chicken

Pork and chicken

Perfectly crisp pork belly

Serves 4
Prep 10 minutes
Cook 2 hours, plus
10 minutes resting

Until now, I'd never managed to get uniformly crisp crackling on my pork belly at the same time as delivering a beautifully cooked, unctuously fatty piece of meat underneath.

Don't bother trying to score the skin with a knife or a blade from the tool box; stabbing the skin with toothpicks takes 2 minutes versus 15 minutes trying to score through the thick skin with even your sharpest knife.

The key to getting that ultra-crisp skin is to mix a little bicarbonate of soda (baking soda) with salt and rub it on to the skin before putting the meat into a cold oven. This allows the pork and the oven to warm together which means unctious fat layers and tender meat. Most importantly, the fat below the skin renders out, leaving the top layer to crisp up. Plus, there's no waiting around for the oven to heat up. Make sure your pork is not fridge-cold when you put it into the oven – take it out of the refrigerator 20–30 minutes before you want to start cooking.

1.5 kg (3lb 5 oz) pork belly
2½ teaspoons fennel seeds, crushed
1 teaspoon dried chilli (hot pepper) flakes
freshly ground black pepper
2 teaspoons fine sea salt
¼ teaspoon bicarbonate of soda (baking soda)

For the sweet-and-sour apple pickles

3 eating (dessert) apples, cored and cut into matchsticks
1½ tablespoons cider vinegar
1½ tablespoons honey
sea salt and freshly ground black pepper

Make sure the surface of your pork is really dry – leave it uncovered in the refrigerator overnight, or use some paper towels to pat the surface dry if necessary. Use a couple of toothpicks or sharp skewers to prick the skin all over as many times as you can, working left to right, right to left, and up and down until it has been pricked many times – you don't want to pierce the skin, simply poke the surface.

Mix the crushed fennel seeds, chilli flakes and some black pepper with 1 teaspoon of the salt, then rub the mixture all over the meat side of the pork belly. Transfer it to a roasting tray (pan). Mix the bicarbonate of soda with the remaining 1 teaspoon of salt, then rub it all over the skin.

Put the tray into a cold oven and set the heat to 180°C/160°C Fan/350°F/Gas 4. Roast the pork for 1½ hours, then increase the oven temperature to 220°C/200°C Fan/430°F/Gas 8 and cook for a further 30 minutes. Remove the pork from the oven, brush off any white sediment that is on the skin and discard. Transfer the pork to a chopping board and allow to rest for 10 minutes.

Meanwhile, make the sweet-and-sour apple pickles. Mix the chopped apples with the vinegar and honey, season and set aside until ready to serve.

To carve the pork, flip it over so it is skin-side down on the chopping board. Use a sharp knife to cut through the meat, then apply some pressure and let the knife break through the crackling. Serve immediately with the pickles.

Make ahead

This can be made 2 days in advance, stored in the refrigerator, then reheated.

The shortcut

Not preheating the oven saves time, and bicarb is a failsafe trick for achieving perfectly crisp skin without having to hang around the grill to monitor its progress.

Beef

lamb

One-dish lasagne

Serves 4, with leftovers
Prep 25 minutes
Cook 1 hour

Can be frozen

Nowadays, I make my lasagne from start to finish in the same large shallow casserole dish (Dutch oven), as I want to keep all of the flavour in one place. Adding a drizzle of cream to the ragu thickens and makes the sauce deliciously rich without lengthy cook times. Gone is the (often lumpy) béchamel sauce, replaced with a mix of creamy ricotta, gooey mozzarella and Parmesan. And to speed the whole thing up, I soak the dried lasagne sheets in warm water before layering. You'll be so chuffed with the lack of washing-up, it's sure to become a regular dinner-time fix.

1 tablespoon olive oil, plus extra
   for drizzling
1 onion, chopped
500 g (1 lb 2 oz) 20 percent fat
   minced (ground) beef
4 garlic cloves, grated
700 g (1 lb 9 oz) passata (sieved
   tomato sauce) with basil
1 teaspoon dried oregano
1 beef or chicken stock cube
200 ml (7 fl oz/scant 1 cup)
   hot water
100 ml (3½ fl oz/scant ½ cup)
   double (heavy) cream, plus
   extra 2 tablespoons
handful of fresh basil leaves
   (optional)
8–12 lasagne sheets (depending
   on size)
250 g (9 oz) ricotta, drained
250 g (9 oz) mozzarella, drained
   and cut into small cubes
75 g (2½ oz) Parmesan, grated
sea salt and freshly ground
   black pepper

Heat the olive oil in a large, shallow, flameproof casserole dish (Dutch oven) over a medium–high heat. Fry the onion for 2 minutes until starting to soften, then add the minced beef. Increase the heat to high and fry for 3 minutes, stirring frequently until the beef has browned all over. Throw in the garlic and fry for 1 minute.

Pour the passata into the dish with the dried oregano and crumble in the stock cube. Fill the passata jar with the hot water, swirl it around, then add to the sauce. Bring the mixture to the boil, then add the 100 ml (3½ fl oz) cream. Tear half of the basil leaves (if using) and add to the sauce with plenty of seasoning. Cook for 5 minutes until the sauce is starting to thicken and look rich in colour, then remove from the heat.

Preheat the oven to 200°C/180°C Fan/400°F/Gas 6. Fill a large bowl with hand-hot water and a drizzle of oil, then slide in the pasta sheets and leave to soak for a few minutes.

Use a ladle to scoop two-thirds of the ragù out into a heatproof bowl. Spread out the remaining third over the base of the casserole dish. In a separate bowl, loosen the ricotta with the extra 2 tablespoons cream and 1 tablespoon of the pasta soaking water.

Lift out and drain enough pasta sheets to cover the surface of the ragu in the casserole dish, laying them gently on top. Spread a third of the ricotta mixture over the pasta, then scatter over a third of the mozzarella and a third of the Parmesan. Add another layer of ragù and repeat until all of the ingredients have been used, finishing with a cheese layer.

Cover the dish with kitchen foil and bake in the hot oven for 15 minutes. Remove the foil and return the dish to the oven for a further 15 minutes, or until the pasta is tender and the lasagne bubbling.

Make ahead

Freeze this, unbaked, for up to 1 month, and defrost overnight before cooking. The meat sauce will keep well in the refrigerator for 1–2 days.

The shortcut

Just 1 pan and no bechamel prep — you're at least 3 hours ahead with your lack of authenticity.

Really smashing burger

Serves 4 or 2
ravenous people
Prep 10 minutes
Cook 5 minutes

I love a good burger, but they are harder to find than you think. I have – in the name of research – eaten many! These couldn't be easier and mean you can have a burger for dinner in 10 minutes.

Smashing the burger into the smoking-hot pan means you get a really good brown crust on the outside. I don't overwork the meat so that the patty is held together but not tough – the meat is juicy, but toothsome, and so good to eat.

Fine sea salt works a treat for seasoning the outside of your burger, but if you only have sea salt flakes, crush them up before you sprinkle – you can do this with the side of a bottle on a wooden board.

I also like to make my own burger sauce. You don't have to, but if you like it you may be tempted to make a big batch. It will happily sit in the refrigerator for a couple of weeks – just give it a good stir before using.

500 g (1 lb 2 oz) 20 percent fat
minced (ground) beef
4 cheese slices (I use strong
Cheddar)
fine sea salt and freshly ground
black pepper

For the burger sauce

4 tablespoons mayonnaise
2 teaspoons tomato ketchup
1 teaspoon Dijon mustard
½ teaspoon smoked paprika
¼ teaspoon garlic powder
(optional)
3 sweet pickles, finely chopped
1 teaspoon pickle juice, from
the jar
fine sea salt and freshly ground
black pepper

To serve

4 burger buns, split
1 little gem (bibb) lettuce, shredded
1 small onion, thinly sliced
1 ripe tomato, sliced
pickles
French fries

First, make the burger sauce. Mix together all the ingredients in a small bowl, then cover and chill until required.

To make the burgers, divide the meat into 4 equal pieces. Gently bring the meat together to form 4 balls, so that the meat is just holding its shape, but is not squashed together.

Heat a large non-stick frying pan (skillet) over a high heat until it is really hot. Drop the meat balls into the pan and carefully flatten, using your fingertips to press down on each one, forming a roughly 10 cm (4 in) patty. Don't worry if the edges are uneven: this will provide delicious crunchy bits of meat. Sprinkle the surface of the meat with a fine, even layer of salt. Fry for 2 minutes, then flip the patties over and season with a little more salt and a twist of pepper.

Top the burgers with a cheese slice and continue to cook for 2 minutes. To fully melt the cheese, add a tablespoon of cold water to the pan and cover with a lid– the steam will help to melt the cheese.

To serve, toast your burger buns under a hot grill (broiler), then spread the buns with the burger sauce. Top each bun with some shredded lettuce, a cheesy burger patty, sliced onion, tomato and pickles. Serve with French fries.

Make ahead

Pre-roll the meat and keep it in the refrigerator, covered, for 2 days – you don't need to bring the meat to room temperature because the pan is smoking hot! The burger sauce will keep in the refrigerator for 2 weeks.

The shortcut

No chopping onions and herbs, or seasoning, or resting. Truly, this is quicker than a takeaway. Get your pan really hot to start cooking and forming that crust immediately – it's where the flavour is.

Beef and lamb

Beef and red wine stew

Serves	4
Prep	15 minutes
Cook	2–2½ hours

Okay, so a really good beef stew does take a long time to cook. There is no getting away from the fact that, in order for the beef to become tender, it needs a decent amount of time on the stove. There are, however, some tricks for speeding the whole thing up; things that I do on photoshoots when I realise I have 3 hours to make a 6-hour stew, small tweaks that speed up the process without sacrificing the final quality of the dish.

Firstly, I brown just one side of the meat really well; the rest, I just colour, which means turning it in the hot pan. I soak my shallots in boiling water so that their papery skins slide off in minutes, rather than taking half an hour to peel. And I don't bother adding in mushrooms and bacon at the end; I add them at the beginning so that everything in the stew gets to cook together, allowing all the flavours to meld and develop – not to mention saving on washing-up. I thicken the stew at the end with a mixture called a *beurre mani*. It sounds fancy, but it's just butter and flour mixed together and whisked into the stew to thicken and give a nice glossy finish. Oh, and I use pre-made mashed potato.

12 shallots
1 tablespoon olive oil
800 g (1 lb 12 oz) stewing steak,
 patted dry with paper towels,
 diced into bite-size pieces
100 g (3½ oz/⅔ cup) smoked
 bacon lardons
200 g (7 oz) button mushrooms
2 garlic cloves, chopped
1 tablespoon balsamic vinegar
2 fresh or dried bay leaves
6 sprigs of thyme, plus extra
 to serve
500 ml (17 fl oz/2 cups) red wine
150 g (5 oz) baby carrots, trimmed
1½ tablespoons butter, softened
1½ tablespoons plain
 (all-purpose) flour
mashed potato, to serve

Put the shallots into a big bowl and cover with boiling water from the kettle. Leave to stand for 10 minutes.

Meanwhile, heat the oil in a large, shallow, flameproof casserole dish (Dutch oven) over a medium-high heat. Add the beef in a single layer and leave for 3 minutes without turning until the bottom of the meat is a dark brown colour and smells delicious. Stir the beef around for 1 minute so that the remaining sides of the meat are lightly coloured, then push the beef to one side.

Drain and peel the shallots and add them to the pan, along with the bacon and mushrooms. Fry for 2 minutes, then stir in the garlic and fry for 1 minute. Add the balsamic vinegar, reduce the heat, then add the herbs and red wine, stirring until everything is well combined. Cover and cook for 1½–2 hours, or until the meat is tender. Add the carrots and continue to cook for a further 8 minutes, or until tender. Mix the butter with the flour in a small bowl and gradually stir the mixture into the stew until you have a thick, glossy sauce. Leave to stand for 5 minutes before serving with mashed potato.

Make ahead

The meat can be browned in advance, and the stew itself will keep well in the refrigerator for 3–4 days. This is also a star of the freezer, where it will keep for 3 months.

The shortcut

You'll save a good 20 minutes by soaking the shallots, and a further 15 minutes by just searing one side of the beef. Adding a thickener to the sauce claws back a good 15 minutes of sauce-reduction time.

Beef and lamb

One-pan spaghetti and meatballs

Serves	4, with leftovers
Prep	5 minutes
Cook	20 minutes

Sometimes, recipes happen because you can stand and dedicate hours to developing them; other times, recipes come about because you have a hungry family who needed feeding an hour ago. And that is how this recipe came about.

Yes, you read that right – one pan for spaghetti and meatballs; every ingredient gets cooked in the same pan. Harnessing all the wonderful flavours from the meatballs that are browned at the start, the pasta then cooks in the tomato sauce releasing its starch directly into the dish, creating a rich, luxurious sauce that clings to the pasta strands. You can also leave the meatballs out and have a pasta with tomato sauce in 10 minutes.

I like to serve this dish with a scattering of crispy pesto-flavoured crumbs. Take the shortest, easiest route to this delicious textural addition and use a packet of store-bought croutons, crushed up – they look great and add a crisp contrast to the tender spaghetti.

olive oil, for frying and drizzling
16 pre-made raw meatballs
    (from the refrigerator section
    in the store)
3 garlic cloves, grated
1 teaspoon dried oregano
½ teaspoon dried chilli
    (hot pepper) flakes
400 g (14 oz) spaghetti
2 x 400 g (14 oz) tins
    chopped tomatoes
1 teaspoon sea salt
25 g (2 oz) Parmesan, finely
    grated, plus extra to serve
handful of basil leaves, chopped
large handful of flavoured
    croutons, crushed (I use basil
    pesto flavour)
freshly ground black pepper

Bring a full kettle or a large saucepan of water to the boil.

Heat 1 tablespoon of oil in a large, shallow, flameproof casserole dish (Dutch oven) or a deep frying pan (skillet) with a metal handle over a medium heat. Fry the meatballs for 8 minutes, turning frequently until browned all over. Remove the meatballs from the pan and set aside, keeping them warm.

Add another drizzle of oil to the dish/pan and fry the garlic for 1 minute, then quickly add the oregano, chilli flakes, spaghetti and tomatoes, scraping the bottom of the pan to lift anything that has caught. Fill both of the tomato tins with boiling water from the kettle and add to the dish/pan, along with the salt and plenty of pepper.

Bring to the boil and cook for 8–10 minutes, stirring every few minutes, until the pasta is just cooked and the sauce is clinging to the strands.

Dot the meatballs over the pasta, submerging them a little in the hot pasta and sauce, then sprinkle with the Parmesan. Scatter over the chopped basil and serve immediately with a drizzle of oil and a scattering of the crushed crispy croutons.

Make ahead

This is so quick, there's no need to make ahead, but you can definitely reheat and eat for lunch or dinner the next day.

The shortcut

Just 20 minutes of cooking time and a single pan – by my reckoning, that's 30 minutes saved on cooking, and another 10 on washing-up.

Beef and lamb

Beef and lamb

Steak and chips with Béarnaise sauce

Serves 2
Prep 10 minutes
Cook 30 minutes

Probably the most important part of making a good steak and chips is getting great-quality beef. Go for a thick cut of steak – sharing makes it feel more celebratory, and with only one to cook, you can focus on getting it right. Season generously all over, including the edges – this ensures flavoursome meat and allows any juices drawn out to be reabsorbed during the coming-to-temperature phase. I know Marmite is divisive, but if you're a fan give it a try – its deeply umami flavour has to be tasted to be believed.

700 g (1 lb 9 oz) bone-in steak, about 4 cm (1½ in) thick (I use T-bone steak)
fine sea salt
a drizzle of light-flavoured oil
2 tablespoons butter
¼ teaspoon Marmite (optional)

For the chips

5 tablespoons light-flavoured oil (I use rapeseed/canola oil)
4 potatoes, peeled and cut into chips about 7.5 mm (⅓ in) thick

For the Béarnaise sauce

75 g (2½ oz/generous ¼ cup) butter
2 large egg yolks
2 teaspoons lemon juice
¼ teaspoon tarragon-flavoured vinegar or white wine vinegar
2 tablespoons hot water
2 tablespoons chopped tarragon or basil
fine sea salt and freshly ground black pepper

Take the steak out of the fridge at least 30 minutes before you are ready to start cooking. Pat the surface dry with paper towels and season generously all over with fine sea salt.

Preheat the oven to 200°C/180°C Fan/400°F/Gas 6.

Start with the chips. Pour the oil into a lipped baking tray (pan) and place in the oven to heat for 10 minutes, or until the oil is really hot. Remove the tray from the oven and carefully lay the chips in the tray an even layer (take care: the hot oil may splutter and spit). Return to the oven and cook for 10 minutes, then remove from the oven and use a spatula to turn the chips over. Return to the oven for another 10 minutes. Drain on paper towels and sprinkle with fine salt.

Meanwhile, heat a heavy-based frying pan (skillet) over a high heat until very hot – you will see the pan begin to smoke slightly. Rub a drizzle of oil over the cut sides of the steak and cook it in the hot pan for 2 minutes – do not move the steak during this time. Flip it over and cook for a further 2 minutes, again leaving it undisturbed. Now cook the steak for a further 2 minutes, flipping it every 15 seconds. Add the butter to the pan, tilt the pan and allow the melted butter to gather at one end. Cook the steak for 1 minute more, turning it every 15 seconds and spooning the melted butter over. Remove the steak from the pan and transfer it to a board. Brush with the Marmite, if using, and spoon over the butter. Leave to stand for 10–15 minutes.

For the Béarnaise sauce, put the butter in a small jug and heat in the microwave for 15–20 seconds or until melted. Beat the egg yolks, lemon juice, vinegar and hot water in a bowl until smooth. Season well, then gradually pour in the melted butter, whisking continuously. Heat in the microwave in 15-second bursts for 1 minute, whisking between each burst until the sauce is thick and smooth. Stir in the chopped tarragon or basil.

Serve the rested steak and hot chips immediately.

Make ahead

Cook the chips in advance and reheat in a hot oven when ready to eat.

The shortcut

Sauce made in the microwave means moments rather than minutes to a dream chip dunking scenario.

Beef and lamb

Lamb pitta kebabs

Serves	2–4
Prep	5 minutes
Cook	15 minutes

These are a cross between a Turkish *lahmacun* (a pizza-like flatbread) and a doner kebab. Flavour-packed, mouth-wateringly juicy, minced (ground) lamb between pockets of soft and crunchy bread – is there any better combination?

Look for lamb with a higher fat content – as I always say, fat is flavour, and you will thank me. As the meat cooks, the juices soak into the bread, creating a soft, pillowy bite on the base of the kebab while the top crisps up.

I use tomato ketchup for a few reasons: it helps to bind the ingredients and it adds a sweet, slightly acidic note to the lamb, which cuts through the richness of the meat. Cooking the meat inside the bread means all of the juices are captured, and it creates a self-contained hand-held dinner.

For the kebabs

200 g (7 oz) minced lamb
½ red onion, grated
1 teaspoon ground cumin
¼ teaspoon dried chilli
   (hot pepper) flakes
1 tablespoon tomato ketchup
handful of flat-leaf parsley,
   roughly chopped
4 round pitta breads
olive oil, for brushing
sea salt and freshly ground
   black pepper

For the onion salad

½ red onion, grated
¼ red cabbage, thinly sliced
juice of ½ lemon
generous pinch of sumac plus
   extra to serve
pinch of salt
handful of flat-leaf parsley,
   roughly chopped
2 tomatoes, halved then sliced
drizzle of olive oil
drizzle of pomegranate
   molasses (optional)

To serve

½ lemon, cut into wedges
plain yoghurt mixed with
   crushed garlic

Put the lamb, onions, spices, ketchup and parsley into the bowl with plenty of seasoning and mix with your hands until combined. Divide the mixture into 4 equal parts, then set aside for 10 minutes for the flavours to come together.

Preheat the oven to 200°C/180°C Fan/400°F/Gas 6.

Meanwhile, start preparing the onion salad. In a bowl mix the onion and red cabbage with the lemon juice, a generous pinch of sumac and some salt. Set aside.

Use a serrated knife to cut the pittas in half – it's easiest if you go around the diameter of each pitta, then lift off the top.

Roll each of the meat portions into a ball and place inside the pitta pockets, squashing them flat so the meat fills the pitta. Transfer the filled pittas to a baking sheet, brush with oil and bake in the oven for 12–15 minutes, or until the meat is cooked through and the pitta golden.

Drain the onion and cabbage mixture, then add the parsley, tomatoes, a glug of olive oil and a drizzle of pomegranate molasses, if using, and mix together. Sprinkle with extra sumac.

Cut the kebabs in half and serve with the onion salad, with the lemon wedges and garlic yoghurt on the side.

Make ahead

You can make the lamb mixture a day in advance, either portioned or unportioned, and store in an airtight container in the refrigerator.

The shortcut

Quicker than a takeaway! And much quicker than firing up the barbecue.

A really good shepherd's pie

Serves 4
Prep 15 minutes
Cook 55 minutes,
plus 10 minutes
cooling

Can be frozen

I use a very Asian trio of flavours in my shepherd's pie, which you might not think is a natural fit in a quintessentially British dish, but trust me – it really works. You will have the ingredients in your storecupboard, and their inherent characteristics can transport even the most traditional British dish to an umami fest. The miso, soy and fish sauce round out the flavours of the dish without overpowering it, making a good dish even more delicious.

Shepherd's pie calls for minced (ground) lamb, but this can be interchanged with minced beef. Lamb is naturally fattier, so if you're using beef, make sure you look out for a mince with twenty percent fat. Remember – fat is flavour! I have to admit, I don't like making mashed potato, so I use store-bought, jazzed up with extra butter and milk. I know many people don't share my disdain for mashing, in which case make your own!

If you don't have a casserole dish that can go in the oven, then transfer the meat to a baking dish before topping it with potato. Just cool the meat first, so the mash doesn't sink.

1 tablespoon olive oil
1 onion, chopped
1 leek, halved lengthways
    and chopped
1 celery stalk, chopped
3 large carrots, diced
2 garlic cloves, grated
2 tablespoons thyme leaves
    or 1 teaspoon dried thyme
500 g (1 lb 2 oz) minced
    (ground) lamb or beef
1 tablespoon plain
    (all-purpose) flour
2 fresh or dried bay leaves
1½ tablespoons miso
1 tablespoon dark soy sauce
1 tablespoon tomato purée (paste)
2 teaspoons fish sauce
200 ml (7 fl oz/scant 1 cup) water
900 g (2 lb) mashed potatoes
    (about 6 large potatoes,
    boiled and mashed)
3 tablespoons whole (full-fat) milk
1 tablespoon butter
100g (3½ oz) strong
    Cheddar, grated

Heat the oil in a large, shallow, flameproof casserole dish (Dutch oven) set over a medium heat. Fry the onion, leek, celery and carrots for 10 minutes, stirring frequently, until starting to soften. Add the garlic and thyme, then push the vegetables to the edge of the pan. Increase the heat, add the meat and fry for 5 minutes until brown, breaking it up with a wooden spoon as you go. Sprinkle over the flour and cook for a further minute.

Throw the bay leaves into the pan, then stir in the miso, soy sauce, tomato purée, fish sauce and water. Bring to a simmer and cook for 20 minutes.

Remove the dish from the heat and allow to cool for about 10 minutes. (You can cool completely and freeze the meat mixture at this point.)

Preheat the oven to 200°C/180°C Fan/400°F/Gas 6.

In a separate saucepan, heat the mashed potato with the milk and butter, stirring until smooth and warmed through.

Top the cooled meat mixture with the mashed potato and rough up the surface with a fork. Scatter over the cheese and cook in the oven for 20 minutes, or until golden and bubbling.

Make ahead

Once assembled, this will sit happily in the refrigerator for 2 days before cooking, and the meat sauce will keep in the freezer for up to 2 months.

The shortcut

A savoury flavour bomb is achieved in minutes with the trio of umami-rich ingredients – trust me, it will taste as though you've slow-cooked it for hours.

Beef and lamb

05

Fish

Fish tacos

Serves 4
Prep 20 minutes
Cook 10 minutes

I use crushed-up salty tortilla chips to form the crispy coating on the outside of my fish tacos. It's such a great shortcut – the chips are seasoned to perfection, they taste great and they provide a brilliant crunch that works so well with the tender, flaky fish inside. You can use whatever flavour of tortilla chips you fancy for this recipe: but before you opt for the extra-spicy variety, just remember that you still want to be able to taste the fish. I serve my fish tacos with a little *curtido*, a chopped cabbage salad. Cabbages can be tricky to chop, so try using a speed peeler; you'll get super-thin, evenly cut shredded cabbage, which will marinade much quicker than the chunky hand-cut variety. You can slice your onions with a speed peeler, too.

150 g (5 oz) salted tortilla chips
1 teaspoon paprika
5 tablespoons plain
   (all-purpose) flour
500 g (1 lb 2 oz) firm white fish,
   defrosted if frozen, cut into
   5 cm (2 in) pieces
light-flavoured oil, for frying
sea salt and freshly ground
   black pepper

For the cabbage salad

¼ red cabbage, shredded
½ red onion, finely sliced
½ teaspoon dried oregano
1 tablespoon cider vinegar
drizzle of light-flavoured oil
sea salt and freshly ground
   black pepper

To serve

12 small tortillas
handful of coriander
   (cilantro) leaves
sour cream
hot sauce

First, make the cabbage salad. In a bowl, mix together the cabbage, onion, oregano and vinegar with a drizzle of oil and plenty of seasoning. Set aside.

Put the tortilla chips in a strong, sealable sandwich bag along with the paprika and bash to fine crumbs – I use a rolling pin and roll over the bag until the chips are crushed. Leave the crumbs in the bag.

Put the flour on a plate and add some seasoning. Flick a little water over the fish so the surface is just glistening but not really wet, then dip the fish pieces in the flour to coat. The water and flour should have made a light batter-like texture on the outside of the fish. Drop the fish into the tortilla crumbs and gently toss to coat all over.

Pour oil into a large non-stick frying pan to a depth of 5 mm (¼ in). Heat over a medium high heat until the oil is hot – the surface of the oil should be simmering. Carefully place the coated fish into the hot oil (in batches if necessary) and cook for 2 minutes, then flip over with a spatula and cook for 1 minute, or until the crumbs are crisp and golden. Remove to a plate and keep warm while you fry the rest.

Wrap the tortillas in foil and warm through in a hot oven for a few minutes. Alternatively, place them (unwrapped) on a microwave-safe plate and heat in the microwave.

Serve the crunchy fish pieces on the tortillas with some cabbage salad, a few coriander leaves and some sour cream and hot sauce, if you like.

Make ahead

The crushed tortilla chips will keep well for a couple of weeks in an airtight bag, but the rest is really a last-minute assembly job.

The shortcut

No breadcrumb blitzing, no deep-frying, but the same amount of crunch – winning.

Quick gravadlax with cucumber salad

Serves	4
Prep	5 minutes, plus minimum 12 hours curing
Cook	No cook

3 x 125 g (4 oz) skin-on salmon fillets (look for the tail-end fillets)
4 tablespoons fine sea salt
4 tablespoons caster (superfine) sugar, plus a pinch
1 teaspoon freshly ground black pepper
6 heaped tablespoons finely chopped dill

For the cucumber salad

1½ tablespoons light-flavoured oil
¾ tablespoons white wine vinegar
½ tablespoon Dijon mustard
¾ tablespoon finely chopped dill
½ cucumber, halved lengthways, seeds removed and sliced
1 sweet dill pickle, thinly sliced
½ small red onion, thinly sliced
sea salt and freshly ground black pepper

To serve

4–8 bagels or rye bread slices
185 g (6½ oz/¾ cup) cream cheese (optional)

I love gravadlax – salty, sweet, dill-cured salmon, thinly sliced and piled on top of fresh bagels or dark rye bread with cucumber salad – it's my idea of heaven.

Here, I use individual salmon fillets, which cure so much faster than a big old side of salmon because the surface area of the fish that is exposed to the salty-sweet cure is maximised. The moisture is drawn out faster, while the sweet-salty-dill flavours permeate the flesh all over. Traditional recipes will call for the fattest part of the fish, but I recommend the thinner tail end. It's all down to that surface-area-to-volume ratio. Do buy sushi-grade salmon or pre-frozen fish (alternatively, you can freeze your salmon and thoroughly defrost it before curing). This is to kill any parasites that might be in the fish.

Pat the salmon dry with paper towels and remove any pin bones with tweezers. Put the salt, sugar, pepper and dill in a large, strong, sealable sandwich bag and mix until fully combined. Put the fillets directly into the cure, flesh-side down, then flip the bag over and make sure all of the fish flesh is covered. Seal the bag, place it in a baking tray, then sit another tray directly on top and weight it down with 3–4 tins of beans. Chill in the refrigerator for 12 hours or overnight.

Unwrap the salmon fillets and use paper towels to remove any surface moisture and to brush off the cure (don't worry about a bit of dill sticking to the fish). Place the salmon on a cutting board and use a sharp knife to cut it into thin slices about 5 mm (¼ in) thick, starting at the widest end. Transfer to a serving plate and discard the skin.

Make the salad dressing in the bowl you're going to serve the salad in. Combine the oil, vinegar, mustard and dill with some seasoning. Whisk to emulsify until the dressing looks yellow and creamy. Add the cucumber, dill pickle and shallot, plus a splash of the pickle juice from the jar. Set aside.

Split and toast the bagels or rye bread, spread with cream cheese, then pile on the sliced gravadlax, cucumber salad and boiled eggs, if using. Serve immediately.

Make ahead

You can cure and slice the salmon, then store it in the refrigerator for 2 days. The cucumber salad can be made an hour in advance

The shortcut

Using thinner, individual fillets means saving a full day of curing time, but it still requires thinking ahead.

Easiest fish pie

Serves 4, with leftovers
Prep 10 minutes
Cook 33 minutes

Fish pie is the epitome of comfort food. What it lacks in looks, it makes up for in taste and texture. I use a fish pie mix containing salmon, pollock (or cod) and smoked haddock. It's easy enough to find and the supermarket has very kindly done all the dirty work for you by chopping it up. I don't bother with a béchamel sauce, opting instead for a mix of double (heavy) cream and fish stock. The little bit of cornflour (cornstarch) used to dust the fish thickens the sauce as the pie cooks, resulting in a rich, velvety, savoury sauce without the hassle of making a béchamel.

Adding a handful of crushed croutons at the end of cooking provides a delicious crunch that works brilliantly with the soft mashed-potato topping. As you'll probably know by now, I don't like mashing potatoes, so I use pre-made store-bought mash, but you can mash your own, if you like.

2 tablespoons butter
6 spring onions (scallions), chopped
2 x 400 g (14 oz) packets fish pie mix
2 teaspoons cornflour (cornstarch)
1 tablespoon Dijon mustard
300 ml (10 fl oz/1¼ cups) double (heavy) cream
200 ml (7 fl oz/scant 1 cup) fish stock
150 g (5 oz) cooked prawns (shrimp)
150 g (5 oz/generous 1 cup) frozen peas, defrosted (optional)
bunch of flat-leaf parsley, roughly chopped
800 g (1 lb 12 oz/3½ cups) pre-cooked mashed potato (if mashing your own, you'll need about 1 kg/2 lb 4 oz potatoes to yield this amount of mash)
50 g (2 oz/½ cup) Parmesan cheese, grated
handful of garlic croutons, bashed to uneven crumbs (optional)
sea salt and freshly ground black pepper

Preheat the oven to 180°C/160°C Fan/350°F/Gas 4.

Put the butter and spring onions in a microwave-safe bowl and microwave for 3 minutes or until soft. Tip out into a 20 x 28 cm (8 x 11 in) baking dish.

Toss the fish pie mix with the cornflour and add to the dish with the spring onions. Combine the mustard, cream, fish stock, prawns, peas, most of the parsley and plenty of seasoning, then add the mixture to the pie dish and gently stir everything together to combine.

Spoon the mashed potato on top of the fish mixture and rough up the surface with a fork. Sprinkle over the Parmesan cheese.

Bake for 30 minutes until the pie is hot through and golden on top. Scatter with the crushed garlic croutons, if using, and the remaining parsley. Serve immediately.

Make ahead

Cool and freeze the pie for up to a month. Defrost and reheat as per the cooking instructions.

The shortcut

Using cream and a little fish stock in place of a béchamel sauce saves you a good 15 minutes.

Ratatouille and sea bass

Serves 4
Prep 10 minutes
Cook 45 minutes

I love those gorgeous, Instagram-worthy dishes of ratatouille, arranged to look like a blooming rose. But while I enjoy looking at them, I don't want to stand there arranging thinly sliced vegetables when I really don't have to. A rustic chop with a sharp knife works just as well and saves you valuable time, plus it's so much easier to get uniformity, which means your vegetables can cook evenly.

I also use pre-roasted peppers from a jar. They are so versatile and convenient – no charred pepper skin stuck to your face, no steaming, no washing up, and so meltingly tender that you don't even need to dirty a knife to chop them up, you can simply tear them into the pan.

Be generous with the olive oil: it adds flavour to the vegetables and helps to form a rich, unctuous sauce.

2 red onions, each cut into 8 wedges through the root
1 aubergine (eggplant), cut into 2 cm (¾ in) cubes
2 courgettes (zucchini), halved lengthways and sliced into half moons
5 garlic cloves, skin on
5 tablespoons olive oil, plus extra for drizzling
1 teaspoon dried oregano
1 tablespoon red wine vinegar, or more as needed
6 tomatoes, quartered
3 roasted red (bell) peppers from a jar, drained and torn into strips
4 sea bass fillets
bunch of fresh basil leaves
sea salt and freshly ground black pepper
good crusty bread, to serve

Preheat the oven to 220°C/200°C Fan/430°F/Gas 8.

Put the onion wedges, aubergine and courgette cubes on a large baking tray (pan) with the garlic, olive oil, oregano, red wine vinegar and plenty of seasoning. Toss everything together to coat with the oil, then spread out into a single layer and roast in the oven for 20 minutes.

Remove the tray from the oven. Take out the garlic cloves and set it aside. Add the tomatoes and roasted peppers to the tray, then return it to the oven for a further 10 minutes.

Meanwhile, pat the fish dry with paper towels and season well with salt and pepper.

Push the garlic from their skins and mash with a little salt and a drizzle of oil.

Pull the vegetables out of the oven, remove about 6 tomato quarters and mash them with the garlic. Stir the garlic-and-tomato mash into the vegetables, then lay the seasoned fish, skin-side up, on top. Drizzle with a little more oil and return the tray to the oven for 8 minutes, or until the fish is just cooked. Taste the veg for seasoning, adding a little more vinegar as required.

Serve the fish and ratatouille immediately, scattered with basil and an extra drizzle of olive oil, with some crusty bread on the side for mopping up the juices.

Make ahead

The ratatouille can be made 3–4 days in advance and kept in the refrigerator, or frozen and eaten within 3 months.

The shortcut

If you cut out the slicing and the roasting of the (bell) peppers, you're saving a good 1½ hours here.

Shrimp burger with Sriracha mayo

Serves 4
Prep 10 minutes
Cook 6 minutes

These shrimp burgers couldn't be easier. Half the prawns (shrimp) are whizzed to a coarse paste and half are roughly chopped: The protein from the whizzed prawns holds the burgers together – no eggs or breadcrumbs required.

I don't shape my shrimp burgers, I simply drop the mixture into the hot oil and then roughly push it out into a burger shape. Doing it this way means you get some nice crunchy bits at the edges, which eat really well.

The Sriracha mayo is optional, but when something tastes this good, why wouldn't you give it a try?

600 g (1 lb 5 oz) raw prawns
(shrimp)
2 spring onions (scallions),
finely chopped
1 red chilli, deseeded and
finely chopped
small handful of coriander
(cilantro), stems and leaves
separated and finely chopped
zest of ½ lime
1 tablespoon light-flavoured oil
sea salt and freshly ground
black pepper

For the Sriracha mayo
2½ tablespoons mayonnaise
1½ tablespoons Sriracha
chilli sauce

To serve
4 sesame-seed buns
handful of rocket (arugula)
1 avocado, peeled and sliced

Put half of the prawns into the bowl of a food processor and pulse a couple of times until roughly chopped, then tip out into a mixing bowl. Add the remaining prawns to the food processor and pulse until a coarse, paste-like texture is achieved. Add to the bowl with the chopped prawns.

Mix in the spring onions, chilli, coriander and the lime zest, along with plenty of seasoning.

Divide the burger mixture into 4 equal parts.

Heat the oil in a large non-stick frying pan (skillet) set over a medium-high heat. When the oil is hot, spoon the portions of burger mixture into the pan and gently flatten to form 4 burger shapes. Fry for 6 minutes, turning halfway through.

Meanwhile, make the Sriracha mayo by simply mixing the mayonnaise and Sriracha sauce together.

Split the buns and toast the cut sides. Spread the buns with spicy mayo, then add a little rocket, some avocado slices and a shrimp burger to each. Chop the zested lime in half, for squeezing, if you like.

Make ahead

+ The burger mix can be made in advance, covered and chilled for up to 2 days.
+ The Sriracha mayo can be made and chilled for up to 1 week.

The shortcut

Whizzing the shrimp to a paste ensures that the proteins hold the burgers together without the need for binders, such as eggs. Scoops of burger mix are fried and roughly shaped in the pan so no fiddly shaping here.

Meat-free

mains

Cacio e pepe

Serves 2
Prep 10 minutes
Cook 10 minutes

Easily doubled

It doesn't get much simpler than *cacio e pepe*. The dish relies on the starchy pasta cooking water, which combines with Parmesan cheese and pepper to form a silky, luxurious taste-bomb of a sauce that clings to the pasta.

If you cook your pasta in a smaller saucepan with less water, the starches in the cooking water become more concentrated, making a beautiful sauce. You can use whatever saucepan you have available to cook your pasta – even a small saucepan will do the trick, although you might have to snap your spaghetti in half so it fits. As always, it's your kitchen ... nobody is checking up on you, so do what you like!

I use only one pan to make my version of cacio e pepe. And while it doesn't get much simpler in terms of ingredients and equipment, I would urge you to prepare everything ahead so you can really get your cooking flow on. From there, it will only take about 10 minutes to have dinner on the table.

sea salt, for the cooking water
200 g (7 oz) spaghetti
    or linguine
large knob of butter
1 teaspoon freshly ground black
    pepper, plus extra to serve
60 g (2 oz) Parmesan
    or pecorino or a mixture
    (or a vegetarian alternative),
    finely grated, plus extra
    to serve

Cook the pasta in a saucepan of boiling, salted water for 6–8 minutes, or until it is not quite tender and still has some bite remaining. Drain and reserve the pasta water.

Quickly return the pan to a medium-high heat. Add the butter and, when melted, add the pepper and heat for about 1 minute until fragrant. Add a ladleful of pasta cooking water (about 100 ml/3½ fl oz/scant ½ cup) to the pan and bring to the boil. Reduce the heat, return the pasta to the pan with three-quarters of the cheese, then stir and shake the pan to melt the cheese and create a sauce that clings to the pasta. Add the remaining cheese and toss the pasta until it melts and you have a silky smooth sauce, adding a splash more of the cooking water if the sauce seems dry.

Divide between warmed dishes and serve immediately with extra cheese and pepper.

Make ahead

You can grate the cheese ahead and store in an airtight container in the refrigerator for 3 days.

The shortcut

This has to be the quickest way to a decadent tasting meal ever. Serve with store-bought garlic bread too, if you like.

My aubergine parmigiana

Serves	4
Prep	10 minutes
Cook	1 hour

If there is anything better than an aubergine parmigiana, it is an easy aubergine parmigiana. Remove the slicing, salting, dipping in egg, frying, dirty plates, dirty fingers, dirty shirt fronts ... it doesn't get any easier than my version.

I use a combination of oil and butter – the butter cooks and adds a delicious creamy, nutty flavour to the final sauce that surrounds your slow-cooked, falling apart, unctuous aubergines (eggplants). It's topped with Parmesan and a few breadcrumbs, I love how some of the cheesy breadcrumbs become soft as they soak up the delicious tomato sauce, while others crisp up. The textural contrasts are just the ticket and hit all the high notes that a traditionally made parmigiana would.

I serve this dish with a big green salad, but if you're not in the mood for salad, try the cooked aubergine stuffed in a hollowed-out crusty baguette – it's the stuff of dreams.

4 medium aubergines (eggplants)
olive oil, for brushing and cooking
large knob of butter, softened
2 x 400 g (14 oz) tins
    chopped tomatoes
2 garlic cloves, grated
1 teaspoon dried oregano
2 x 125 g (4 oz) balls mozzarella,
    cubed
30 g (1 oz) Parmesan, finely grated
large handful of fresh breadcrumbs
large handful of basil leaves,
    (optional)
sea salt and freshly ground
    black pepper

Preheat the oven to 200°C/180°C Fan/400°F/Gas 6.

Make deep slits, 1 cm (½ in) apart, across each of the aubergines, making sure you don't cut all of the way through. Use a pastry brush to coat the inside of the cuts with oil. Dot the butter over each of the aubergines and season inside and out.

Mix together the tomatoes, garlic, oregano and some seasoning – I usually do this in the tomato tins. Pour the tomato mixture into a 20 x 30 cm (8 x 12 in) baking dish and sit the aubergines on top. Cover with kitchen foil and cook in the oven for 50 minutes, or until the aubergines are starting to get really soft.

Remove the dish from the oven and remove the foil. Use the back of a spoon to open up the aubergine cuts and stuff with cubes of mozzarella and some of the tomato sauce. Sprinkle over the Parmesan and breadcrumbs, then return the dish to the oven and cook uncovered for a final 10 minutes, or until the breadcrumbs are golden.

Leave to stand for 5 minutes, then scatter with basil (if using) before serving.

Make ahead

Prep the whole dish in advance and reheat in a hot oven until piping hot.

The shortcut

All the textural expectations of a parmigiana, none of factory line-style crumbing. No salting, no dipping in egg, no frying in oil. One pan, no-hassle cooking.

Meat-free mains

Tomato and ricotta galette

Serves	4
Prep	15 minutes
Cook	30–40 minutes

This is a free-form tart, which is beautiful brought to the table whole, piled with bursting tomatoes. Sundried tomatoes seemed to go out of fashion some time ago, but if – like me – you still enjoy their intense flavour and always have a jar in the refrigerator, you'll be pleased to see this recipe calls for their chewy, almost meaty texture and rich tomatoey flavour.

I add thyme and Parmesan to store-bought pastry so that their flavour infuses as it cooks. If you have ever made Portuguese custard tarts, you'll recognise the method I use to roll out the pastry – the layers of the pastry stand vertically rather than horizontally, giving an extra-crisp edge.

150 g (5 oz) mixed cherry tomatoes
plain (all-purpose) flour, for dusting
320 g (11 oz) all-butter puff pastry sheet
2 tablespoons thyme leaves
50 g (2 oz ½ cup) Parmesan, finely grated
250 g (9 oz) ricotta cheese, drained
3 large eggs
8 sundried tomatoes in oil, finely chopped, some of the oil reserved for drizzling
sea salt and freshly ground black pepper

To halve the cherry tomatoes, put them all on a chopping board and cover with a flat lid or another light chopping board. Use a large serrated knife to cut through the middle of every tomato in one movement. Set aside.

Unroll the puff pastry on a lightly floured work surface. Sprinkle over half of the thyme leaves and half of the Parmesan, lightly pushing them into the pastry. Roll the pastry up into a long sausage shape, then curl the pastry sausage up like a snail. Use a rolling pin to roll the pastry out into a 30 cm (12 in) circle. Transfer to a lined baking sheet.

Preheat the oven to 200°C/180°C Fan/400°F/Gas 6 and put a second baking sheet in the oven to heat up.

Mix the remaining thyme and Parmesan with the ricotta and 2 of the eggs and season well. Scatter half of the sundried tomatoes over the centre of the pastry base, leaving a border of about 4 cm (1½ in), then spoon the ricotta mixture over the top. Quickly fold up the edges of the pastry to enclose the filling. Beat the remaining egg and brush the edge of the pastry.

Remove the preheated tray from the oven and slide the galette onto the hot tray using the paper to move it from one to the other – this will help to cook the pastry base. Bake for 20 minutes, then remove from the oven and place the halved tomatoes on top. Return to the oven and continue to cook for 15 minutes. Check the base is cooked and golden – if it isn't, cover the top of the galette lightly with foil and continue baking for 5–10 minutes, or until golden and crisp.

Scatter the remaining sundried tomatoes over the top.

Make ahead

This is best warm from the oven, but also fairs well in lunchboxes, so it's worth keeping back a piece for the next day, or cooking specifically to eat throughout the week.

The shortcut

Store-bought pastry with added flavour and the use of sundried tomatoes will make this taste – and look – like the makings of a deli, when actually your prep time is 15 minutes at most.

Meat-free mains

Custardy macaroni cheese

Serves 6–8, with leftovers
Prep 10 minutes
Cook 35 minutes,
plus 5 minutes
standing

Custardy and custody: two words that spring to my mind with this dish. Custody of this dish belongs firmly in the hands of my beloved, and he has very kindly said that I can use it here. This macaroni cheese is like no other (unless, of course, you make yours like this, too!).

And custardy is the only way I can describe this unapologetically cheesy, A-mazing dish. Macaroni cheese is traditionally served up as a side dish, but I will happily eat as a main with some side salad, or a dollop of ketchup. It is also perfect with a roast chicken dinner – yes, trust me. Or a big old juicy steak.

This makes quite a big dish, but I urge you to make it all, even if you're only serving two, and then eat the leftovers warmed up in the oven until hot and crispy. A cross between the best quiche you have ever eaten and the most satisfying baked cheesy pasta dish you've ever been lucky enough to devour – you will want leftovers. I have been known to eat this for breakfast, lunch and dinner.

This is such a simple dish – cooked pasta layered up with cheese and submerged in a creamy custard sauce made with eggs and evaporated milk. It's so much easier and quicker than a roux-based macaroni cheese. You want a few little macaroni to be sticking up out of the top of the dish, as these become deliciously crunchy and work so well with the soft pasta beneath.

500 g (1 lb 2 oz) elbow macaroni
butter, for greasing
200 g (7 oz) extra-mature
Cheddar cheese, cubed
200 g (7 oz) gruyère, grated
250 g (9 oz) pre-grated mozzarella
2 x 410 g (14½ oz) tins
evaporated milk
4 eggs, lightly beaten
1 tablespoon Dijon mustard
pinch of cayenne pepper
sea salt and freshly ground
black pepper

Bring a large saucepan of salted water to the boil and cook the macaroni pasta for 2 minutes less than the packet instructions. Drain and cool under cold running water, then drain again.

Preheat the oven to 180°C/160°C Fan/350°F/Gas 4.

Grease a large, deep 20 x 30 cm (8 x 12 in) baking dish with butter and tip a third of the cooked macaroni into the dish. Scatter over a third of each of the cheeses, then cover with another layer of macaroni. Continue layering until you have 3 layers of pasta, ending with a layer of cheese.

In a large bowl, mix the evaporated milk with the eggs, mustard and cayenne pepper, and season with 1 teaspoon salt and plenty of pepper. Pour the mixture over the pasta and cheese, then use the end of a fork to wiggle it around in the pasta to help distribute the custard.

Bake in the oven for 30 minutes until the dish is set and the top is golden. Leave to stand for 5 minutes before serving.

Make ahead

This cries out to be made ahead, given that the leftovers are almost better. Keep it in the refrigerator uncooked for 48 hours, or cooked for up to 4 days.

The shortcut

Joy of joys, no béchamel to make!

Meat-free mains

Sweet potato ravioli with sage and brown butter

Serves 2
Prep 10 minutes
Cook 25 minutes

Making your own pasta for ravioli is fun, but can be time consuming. This is the ultimate shortcut, using lasagne sheets simply boiled until soft and folded over to enclose the rich, sweet and savoury sweet potato filling. Frying the ravioli crisps up the outside of the pasta, which works wonderfully with the soft, creamy filling. One of my favourite things about this dish is that it looks rather fancy and would definitely pass as a sophisticated dinner party meal.

I use sweet potato because I find squash and pumpkin can be difficult to work with when you're time poor and you're looking for a quick meal. A sweet potato does the trick perfectly and is easy to handle – it can be peeled, chopped and cooked in minutes and tastes every bit as delicious.

Crisp, fried sage is the perfect finish to this dish. It adds a great texture and the taste of sage fried in brown butter is sublime – fry up a few extra to nibble on with some flaky salt.

1–2 sweet potatoes, about 500 g
  (1 lb 2 oz), cut into 1 cm
  (½ in) cubes
50 g (2 oz/½ cup) Parmesan,
  finely grated
fresh nutmeg, for grating
pinch of ground cinnamon
6 dried pre-cooked lasagne sheets
olive oil, for cooking and drizzling
4 tablespoons butter
24 sage leaves
sea salt and freshly ground
  black pepper

Put the sweet potato(es) into a heatproof bowl with 1 tablespoon of water, cover with cling film (plastic wrap) and cook in the microwave on high for 3–5 minutes, or until very tender, checking halfway through. Drain off any excess liquid and mash with a fork. Add two-thirds of the Parmesan to the bowl, along with a generous grating of nutmeg and the cinnamon. Season to taste and set aside.

Bring a large frying pan (skillet) of salted water to the boil. Add the pasta and a drizzle of oil to stop the sheets sticking, then cook for 12 minutes, or for 2 minutes longer than the packet instructions. Drain and separate the sheets, then let cool for a few minutes.

Cut each lasagne sheet in half with kitchen scissors, so you have 12 squares. Dollop 1 tablespoon of the sweet potato mixture into the middle of each square and top each one with a sage leaf. Fold the pasta over the filling to form a rough triangle and press to seal the edges together. Leave to cool on a lightly oiled tray.

Dry the pan and return it to a high heat, then add the butter and a splash of oil. When the butter is foaming, add the remaining sage leaves and cook until they are dark green and crisp. Remove and set aside. Add the cooled ravioli to the pan and cook for 2 minutes on each side until golden at the edges and crisp. Divide between 2 plates and serve with the remaining Parmesan, sage leaves and a drizzle of olive oil.

Make ahead

The filling can be made up to 2 days in advance and chilled. The assembled ravioli will sit happily in the fridge on a lightly oiled tray for 2 days.

The shortcut

Using lasagne sheets means these ravioli can be whipped up any day of the week – no fresh pasta making here – while the sweet potato filling is made in minutes when you use the microwave.

Oven-baked creamy garlic mushroom risotto

Serves 4
Prep 10 minutes, plus 10 minutes soaking
Cook 30 minutes

I want to be able to eat a great flavour-packed, oozy risotto whenever I fancy, not whenever I have the time to stand at the stove for a good chunk of my evening, stirring and ladling. This oven-baked risotto is great because, after a few minutes on the stovetop, the oven does all of the hard work. Use a combination of dried porcini, which add masses of intense mushroom flavour and bring a nice texture to the risotto, and fresh chestnut (cremini) mushrooms, which become silky and soft as they cook in the dish. I use a nice garlic and herb soft cheese to add a pop of creamy brightness to the dish, but if you'd prefer to use mascarpone or soft cheese, they will work well, too.

30 g (1 oz) dried porcini mushrooms
2 tablespoons olive oil, plus extra to serve
2 tablespoons butter
1 onion, finely chopped
250 g (9 oz) chestnut (cremini) mushrooms, sliced
2 garlic cloves, grated
1 tablespoon thyme leaves, plus extra to serve
350 g (12 oz) risotto rice
800 ml (27 fl oz/3¼ cups) hot vegetable stock
75 g (2½ oz) garlic and herb soft cheese (I use Boursin)
30 g (1 oz) Parmesan, finely grated
sea salt and freshly ground black pepper

Put the porcini mushrooms in a bowl and cover with 500 ml (17 fl oz/2 cups) boiling water from the kettle. Leave to stand for 10 minutes.

Meanwhile, preheat the oven to 200°C/180°C Fan/400°F/ Gas 6.

Heat the olive oil and butter in a large flameproof and ovenproof casserole dish over a medium–high heat, then add the onion and plenty of seasoning and cook for 2 minutes. Add the chestnut mushrooms and garlic, and cook for 3 minutes, stirring frequently, until the mushrooms are starting to soften.

Drain the porcini mushrooms, reserving the liquid, and roughly chop. Stir the chopped porcini, thyme and rice into the pot, then pour in the porcini soaking liquid and hot stock and bring to the boil.

Remove from the heat, cover and bake in the hot oven for 25 minutes, or until the rice is cooked but still has a little bite. Stir in the garlic and herb soft cheese and most of the Parmesan, adjusting the seasoning to taste.

Serve scattered with extra thyme leaves, the remaining Parmesan and a drizzle of olive oil.

Make ahead

You can soak the mushrooms and then soften the rest up to a day ahead. It's also worth noting that any leftovers can be rolled into little patties and pan-fried – an excellent base for a poached egg.

The shortcut

No stirring, which means you can spend 25 minutes doing anything but.

Meat-free mains

Raclette-ish

Serves 2
Prep 5 minutes
Cook 15 minutes

If there is one positive to cold weather, it is that you get to embrace the full-bodied, full-fat, carb-and-cheese-fest that is raclette, while wearing clothes that cover a whole multitude of sins. I love those little kits you can buy that sit on the tabletop, where you scrape cheese from a hot plate on to your cooked potatoes, but frankly I sometimes just want to dig in and keep eating until I am only good for a nap. This is a great dish for sharing and is somewhere between a fondue, with its oozy cheese, a tartiflette, with its layers of potatoes and onions, and – of course – raclette's molten coverage of all that it touches.

For this recipe, the onions should not be raw but should not be cooked either, so they maintain a little bite and fresh flavour. The method I use here achieves the perfect balance. Pouring the cooked potatoes and their cooking water over the sliced onions removes their natural bitterness and rounds out the rawness without cooking.

Squashing the potatoes lightly provides craggy texture, which gets crisp under the hot grill when smothered in cheese. This is really just a quick assembly dish with minimal cooking. It's great to share with a friend, or halve the recipe and indulgently enjoy alone. Serve with a bitter leaf salad such as endive.

300 g (10½ oz) baby
   new potatoes
½ small onion, thinly sliced
4 tablespoons crème fraîche
1 teaspoon Dijon mustard
150 g (5 oz) raclette cheese,
   pre-sliced
sea salt and freshly ground
   black pepper
cornichons, to serve

For the endive salad

1 tablespoon olive oil
½ teaspoon white wine vinegar
¼ teaspoon Dijon mustard
¼ garlic clove, crushed
2 heads endive, broken into leaves
1 tangerine, peeled and chopped
sea salt and freshly ground
   black pepper

Cook the potatoes in a saucepan of boiling salted water for 10 minutes or until really tender. Put the chopped onions in a sieve, then drain the cooked potatoes directly over the top. Leave to steam dry.

Meanwhile, preheat the grill (broiler) to high.

Put the potatoes and onions into an ovenproof frying pan (skillet) or sauté pan. Crush the potatoes lightly with the back of a spoon to break them apart slightly – you want them to have a rough surface texture.

Stir the crème fraîche and mustard together in a bowl with some seasoning. Spoon the mixture all over the potatoes and onions, then top with the raclette slices. Cook under the hot grill for 3–5 minutes, or until the cheese is molten.

To make the salad, add the olive oil, vinegar, mustard and garlic to a serving bowl, season, then whisk to combine. Add the endive leaves and tangerine and toss to coat.

Serve the raclette-ish with the salad and cornichons.

ke ahead

ing can be made 2–3 days in advance and stored
  ly in the refrigerator until assembly time.

The shortcut

No waiting for individual servings of raclette to melt.

Meat-free mains

Saag paneer with kachumba salad

Serves 4
Prep 10 minutes
Cook 25 minutes

This is my go-to Indian takeaway order, but I am often left disappointed by what I get, so I came up with my own super-easy version, which means consistency every time.

I make a spice mix to coat and marinade the paneer – it forms a delicious crust on the cheese and forms the basis of the spinach sauce. The frozen spinach really does the rest of the work and creates a smooth, delicious, fresh base.

1 tablespoon ground cumin
2 teaspoons ground turmeric
1½ teaspoons chilli powder
1½ teaspoons ground coriander
generous pinch of salt
2 x 250 g (9 oz) packs paneer,
    cut into 2 cm (¾ in) cubes
light-flavoured oil, for frying
1 onion, finely chopped
1 green chilli, chopped
3 garlic cloves, grated
handful of coriander (cilantro),
    leaves and stalks separated
    and chopped
500 g (1 lb 2 oz) frozen spinach
100 ml (3½ fl oz/scant ½ cup)
    double (heavy) cream

For the kachumba salad

½ cucumber, halved lengthways
4 ripe tomatoes, halved
½ small onion, finely chopped
pinch of cumin seeds, bashed
sea salt and freshly ground
    black pepper

For the mint sauce

150 g (5 oz/⅔ cup) plain yoghurt
2 teaspoons shop-bought
    mint sauce
sea salt and freshly ground
    black pepper

To serve

mango chutney, naan bread
    or chapatti and/or rice

First, make the kachumba salad. Use a teaspoon to scoop the seeds out of the cucumber and tomatoes, then finely chop them into small dice. Transfer to a bowl, along with the onion and cumin seeds. Season and mix together. Set aside.

In a separate bowl, make the mint sauce. Mix together the yoghurt and mint sauce with some seasoning, and set aside.

In a medium mixing bowl, mix together the ground spices with a generous pinch of salt. Tip half of the spice mix out into a small bowl and set aside. Lightly wet your hands with water, then toss the paneer in the remaining spice mix until well coated (the water from your hands will help the spices stick to the paneer).

Heat a generous glug of oil in a large non-stick frying pan (skillet) with a lid set over a medium–high heat. Add the paneer and cook on all sides for 2–3 minutes, turning frequently, until golden and a crust has formed. Remove from the pan and set aside.

Add a tablespoon of oil to the pan, then add the onion and fry for 3 minutes until starting to soften. Tip in the chilli, garlic, coriander stalks and the remaining spice mix, and fry for 1 minute, or until fragrant.

Dot the frozen spinach over the surface of the pan, cover the pan with the lid and cook for 12 minutes, stirring halfway through. Stir in the cream, return the paneer to the pan, and heat through.

Serve with the kachumba salad and mint sauce, along with some mango chutney and bread or rice, if you like.

Make ahead

You can coat the paneer in the spice mix up to a day ahead and keep it in the refrigerator – even better flavours will develop. This is great reheated and can be made up to 2 days in advance.

The shortcut

Using frozen spinach means no washing leaves, no wilting, and no blitzing to a sauce – quicker to make than to order a takeaway. The added mint sauce and salad helps to get the takeaway feel at home.

Meat-free mains

Beetroot and mushroom bourguignon

Serves 4
Prep 15 minutes
Cook 35 minutes

This vegan version of the French classic is super speedy to prepare and cooks in the time it would take just to brown the beef of its meaty counterpart. You won't be disappointed with the rich, warming stew, especially when served with mashed potatoes.

The starting point is making 'vegan bacon', which has a great texture and smoky taste. Make extra and serve on toast with avocado.

For the 'vegan bacon'

olive oil, for frying
200 g (7 oz) chestnut (cremini) mushrooms, thinly sliced
1 teaspoon sweet smoked paprika
¼ teaspoon garlic powder
1 tablespoon maple syrup

For the stew

olive oil, for frying and drizzling
2 onions, chopped
2 carrots, sliced diagonally
4 portobello mushrooms, thickly sliced
3 garlic cloves, chopped
1 tablespoon thyme leaves, plus extra to serve
1 tablespoon tomato purée (paste)
1 tablespoon plain (all-purpose) flour
375 ml (12½ fl oz 1½ cups) full-bodied red wine
1 vegetable stock cube
150 ml (5 fl oz/scant ⅔ cup) water
1 bay leaf
8 cooked beetroots (beets), cut into wedges
sea salt and freshly ground black pepper

To serve

mashed potato

To make the 'vegan bacon', heat a drizzle of oil in a large non-stick frying pan (skillet) with a lid, set over a high heat. Fry the chestnut mushrooms in a single layer for 1–2 minutes on each side until golden and most of the liquid has evaporated. You may need to do this in batches. Remove the cooked mushrooms to a plate lined with paper towels and continue frying the rest.

Return all the mushrooms to the frying pan, then sprinkle over the paprika, garlic powder and maple syrup. Stir to coat and fry for 1 minute. Remove from the heat, tip the mushrooms on to a plate and set aside.

Next, make the stew. Return the pan to a medium heat, add a glug of oil, then fry the onions and carrots for 5–8 minutes until starting to soften. Push these to one side, turn up the heat, add a little more oil and fry the portobello mushrooms for 3 minutes. Tip in the garlic and thyme and fry for 1 minute, then stir in the tomato purée with plenty of seasoning.

Sprinkle in the flour, then stir in the red wine. Finally, crumble in the stock cube, add the water, drop in the bay leaf and add the beetroot wedges. Cover the pan with the lid and cook for 15 minutes.

Just before serving, stir in most of the 'vegan bacon', reserving some to sprinkle on top. Serve with mashed potato and a sprinkling of thyme leaves and a drizzle of oil.

Make ahead

This will happily sit in the refrigerator for 3–4 days, and will freeze well for up to 3 months. It's a good one to batch-cook and freeze in portions to defrost on lazy days.

The shortcut

Beetroot can be a faff to prepare and messy to boot. In this recipe, I use pre-cooked vac-packed beetroot to save a good hour – just make sure it isn't pickled in vinegar.

Meat-free mains

A really good vegan chilli with quick pickles

Serves 4, with leftovers
Prep 15 minutes
Cook 30 minutes

This chilli is tried and tested by vegans, vegetarians and die-hard carnivores alike. It tastes like it has been on the stovetop for hours, but in reality it can be on the table within thirty minutes, with homemade pickles on the side. It's a great all rounder.

The hack to this dish is lifting out a cup of the cooked beans and mash them up, then return them to the pot for a luxurious creaminess. Pulling out a spoonful of the cooked onion and garlic to stir back in at the end also builds a really rich flavour profile.

For the bean chilli

2 tablespoons olive oil
2 onions, roughly chopped
4 garlic cloves, roughly chopped
1 bunch coriander (cilantro),
    leaves and stalks separated
    and chopped
1 tablespoon smoked paprika
1 tablespoon ground cumin
2 teaspoons dried oregano
1½ teaspoons ground cinnamon
1 teaspoon dried chilli (hot
    pepper) flakes
2 x 400 g (14 oz) tins kidney beans
400 g (14 oz) tin black eyed beans
400 g (14 oz) tin black beans
400 g (14 oz) tin chopped tomatoes
50 g (2 oz) dairy-free dark
    chocolate, roughly chopped
sea salt and freshly ground
    black pepper

For the pickles

juice of 1 lime
1 teaspoon sugar
½ teaspoon salt
1 small red onion, thinly sliced
2 carrots, cut into long strips
    with a julienne peeler

To serve

boiled rice or baked sweet
    potatoes
dairy-free yoghurt

First, make the pickles. Put the lime juice, sugar and salt into a bowl and stir until the sugar has dissolved. Add the onion and carrots and toss to combine. Set aside.

For the chilli, heat the oil in a large heavy-based flameproof casserole dish (Dutch oven) over a medium–high heat. Add the onions, garlic and coriander stalks and fry for 5 minutes until starting to soften. Remove a large spoonful of the onion mixture to a bowl and set aside. Add the spices to the casserole dish and fry for 1 minute. Drain all but one of the tins of beans, and tip them into the pan with the reserved bean liquid. Stir in the tomatoes. Bring to a simmer and cook for 20 minutes.

Ladle a large cup of beans out of the pan and add to the reserved onion mixture. Tip this into the bowl of a food processor and whizz until smooth and creamy. Add the mixture back into the chilli, along with the chopped chocolate, and stir until melted. Taste for seasoning.

Spoon the chilli into bowls, and serve with rice or baked sweet potatoes, the pickles, a dollop of yoghurt and the coriander leaves.

Make ahead

This will keep well in both the refrigerator and freezer; about 1 week for the former, and 3 months for the latter.

The shortcut

No bean-soaking required, which means you can even eat this winter warmer on a whim.

Desserts

Apple pie

Serves 6
Prep 25 minutes
Cook 40–45 minutes

**Can be frozen
before cooking**

500 g (1 lb 2 oz) block all-butter
    shortcrust pastry
5 tablespoons Demerara sugar,
    plus extra for sprinkling
2 teaspoons ground cinnamon,
    plus an extra pinch
1 egg white, beaten with a fork
6 eating (dessert) apples,
    peeled, cored and sliced (I use
    3 Granny Smiths and 3 Gala)
3 tablespoons caster
    (superfine) sugar
2 tablespoons cornflour
    (cornstarch)
1 tablespoon cider vinegar
whipped cream, to serve

I love apple pie at any time. My current favourite is this pastry-pinwheel-topped creation with cinnamon and brown sugar. So delicious to eat – like your favourite apple pie, made better. Think crisp, buttery, cinnamon sugary palmiers atop a juicy, appley middle, with a hint of cider vinegar to guarantee an intense sweet and tart apple flavour. It's just so pretty: you will look as though you've made masses of effort. Genius!

Preheat the oven to 180°C/160°C Fan/350°F/Gas 4. Line a baking sheet with baking parchment.

Divide the pastry in half. Setting one half aside for the pinwheels, roll the other half into a ball, then roll it out to a circle large enough to line a pie dish roughly 22 cm (8½ in) wide and 4 cm (1¾ in) deep. Trim off any excess pastry from around the edges and save it for the pinwheels. Chill the lined pie dish in the refrigerator for 15 minutes.

Meanwhile, make the cinnamon sugar pinwheels. Mix the Demerara sugar and 2 teaspoons of ground cinnamon in a small bowl and set aside. Roll out the other pastry half and any off-cuts to form a 20 x 15 cm (8 x 6 in) rectangle. Brush the surface of the pastry with egg white then sprinkle the cinnamon sugar over the surface of the pastry, then roll up the rectangle into a long, thin sausage shape. Use a sharp knife to cut the pastry sausage into 5 mm (¼ in) discs. Lay the discs cut-side up and gently roll them out with a rolling pin, or the side of a clean bottle, to circles about 5 cm (2 in) in diameter. Transfer the pinwheels to the lined baking sheet and chill in the refrigerator for a few minutes.

In a bowl, mix the apples with the remaining pinch of cinnamon, caster sugar, cornflour and cider vinegar, and stir to combine. Pile the apples into the pastry-lined pie dish. Brush the rim of the pastry with a little of the egg white. Lay the pinwheels on top of the apple filling, starting at the outer rim of the pastry and working into the middle. Don't worry if there are a few gaps, as this will allow steam to escape. Brush the surface of the pinwheels with egg white and sprinkle with the extra Demerara sugar.

Bake in the hot oven for 40–45 minutes until golden. Serve warm, with whipped cream.

Make ahead

+ You can prep the pastry a couple of days in advance and chill in the refrigerator.
+ The pie freezes well, uncooked, for up to 1 month. Defrost before cooking as instructed.

The shortcut

Stunning, flavour-infused pastry with none of the crumbling, kneading, chilling and rolling that's usually required.

Plum tarte tatin

Serves 6
Prep 15 minutes
Cook 25 minutes

The idea of flipping over a tarte tatin on to a serving plate and seeing the soft, sticky fruit fall perfectly into place atop a crisp puff pastry disc is wonderful. The reality, however, is often not so good. Failed attempts at caramel, either burnt and stuck to the sides of your pan, or crystallised into a mass and, again, welded to your freshly washed pan, can have you thinking that maybe tarte tatin can only be enjoyed in a restaurant or longingly ogled at in a cookbook.

This tried and tested recipe is one of my go-to, superstar, show-off desserts and, until now, I haven't shared my secret. I have soaked up the praise and glory piled on me, and eaten joyfully in the knowledge that I have used just four ingredients to create a gem of a dessert that never fails to impress. And it has never once had me soaking burnt caramel off my pans.

25 g (1 oz) butter, softened
7–8 firm, ripe plums, halved
 and stones removed
320 g (11 oz) sheet ready-rolled
 puff pastry
plain (all-purpose) flour, for dusting
4 tablespoons store-bought
 caramel sauce or dulce
 de leche
good-quality vanilla ice cream,
 to serve

Preheat the oven to 200°C/180°C Fan/400°F/Gas 6.

Spread the butter over the base of a 20 cm (8 in) ovenproof frying pan (skillet) in an even layer. Place the plums, cut-side down, into the butter.

Unroll the puff pastry on to a floured work surface and cut it into a rough 24 cm (9½ in) disc, or just bigger than your frying pan. Lay the pastry disc on top of the plums and tuck the edges down the sides of the pan.

Bake in the oven for 25 minutes until the pastry is golden-brown and risen. Leave to cool for 5 minutes in the pan. (Put a dish towel over the handle so you remember the pan is hot!)

Gently heat the caramel in a small saucepan or in a bowl in the microwave for 1–2 minutes to loosen. To turn the tarte tatin out, put a serving plate on top of the pastry, hold the plate with one hand and the pan with the other. Quickly flip the pan upside down and carefully lift it off. The plums should be facing cut side up – if they're not rearrange. Spoon over the caramel, letting it fall in between the soft plums.
Cut the tarte tatin into wedges and serve immediately with ice cream.

Make ahead

Prep your plums a few hours before you need them, add a squeeze of lemon juice to stop them going brown and store, cut-side down on a plate in the refrigerator.

The shortcut

Shhhhh ... don't bother making caramel, use a tin of store-bought caramel sauce.

Desserts

Self-saucing sticky toffee pudding

Serves	6–8
Prep	20 minutes
Cook	45 minutes

If I see sticky toffee pudding on a menu, I am only going through the motions of eating the main course in order to get to dessert faster, lest I be told 'we've sold out of the sticky toffee pudding'. It's happened to me so many times that I came up with this self-saucing recipe to streamline and speed up my own version of the pud.

What happens as this pudding cooks is nothing short of miraculous. As the cake bakes and rises, the wet ingredients sink to the bottom of the dish, making a rich toffee sauce which puddles underneath the sponge. No separate sauce-making required. Serve this soon after removing it from the oven, or the sauce will be reabsorbed.

100 g (3½ oz/generous ⅓ cup) butter, melted, plus extra for greasing
175 g (6 oz/generous 1 cup) soft dried pitted dates, chopped
75 ml (2½ fl oz/5 tablespoons) boiling water
200 ml (7 fl oz/scant 1 cup) milk
3 large eggs, lightly beaten
75 g (2½ oz/scant ½ cup) soft dark brown sugar
75 g (2½ oz/⅓ cup) caster (superfine) sugar
300 g (10½ oz/2⅓ cups) self-raising (self-rising) flour
1 teaspoon baking powder
¼ teaspoon mixed spice
ice cream or cream, to serve

For the sticky toffee sauce
300 ml (10 fl oz/1¼ cups) boiling water
150 g (5 oz/generous ¾ cup) soft dark brown sugar
5 tablespoons double (heavy) cream
pinch of salt

Preheat the oven to 180°C/160°C Fan/350°F/Gas 4.

Grease a deep rectangular baking dish, 20 x 28 cm (8 x 11 in), with butter and place it on top of a baking sheet. Bring a kettle or a large pan of water to the boil.

Put the chopped dates into a jug and cover with the 75 ml (2½ fl oz/5 tablespoons) boiling water. Leave to stand for 5 minutes or until softened, then use a hand-held stick blender to process until smooth. Add the melted butter, milk and eggs to the dates and stir to combine.

Put both types of sugar, flour, baking powder and mixed spice into a large mixing bowl. Pour in the date mixture and stir to combine. Scrape the mixture into the baking dish and smooth the surface with the back of a spoon.

Next, make the sticky toffee sauce. Measure out the 300 ml (10 fl oz/1¼ cups) boiling water in a measuring jug, then add the sugar, cream and a good pinch of salt. Stir until the sugar and salt have dissolved, then quickly pour the mixture all over the cake batter. Bake in the oven for 45 minutes until the top is set and the sauce is bubbling up around the edges.

Carefully remove the pudding from the oven and leave to stand for 5 minutes, then scoop out portions and serve with ice cream or cream.

Make ahead

+ You can prepare the wet ingredients a few hours before you want to make the pudding, then just mix with the dry ingredients and continue as per usual.
+ Get a jug of the ingredients for the magic sauce ready to go when you prep the dry and wet ingredients and top up with boiling water from the kettle. This can't be reheated in the oven, but a very short blast in the microwave will warm the sponge and make the sauce softer again.

The shortcut

As the pudding makes its own sauce, you are free from the additional faff of preparing the sticky-toffee element.

Desserts

Peach and blueberry crumble

Serves 4
Prep 10 minutes
Cook 30 minutes

I had never really been a frozen-aisle dweller, preferring 'fresh' even if it was out of season. But now, I am a convert: frozen fruit and vegetables are, for the most part, frozen at the point of harvest and at the peak of ripeness, so you will always have fruit bursting with flavour. For this recipe, I also use tinned peaches, firstly because they are always sweet and ripe, and secondly because the juice in the tin becomes a sauce for your fruit to cook in.

Rich, buttery shortbread biscuits (cookies) take the place of a traditional crumble topping, so you don't even have to get your hands messy rubbing in butter. The trick is to bash your shortbread to an uneven rubble, so you have a great mix of texture. This looks and tastes as good as any 'from scratch' crumble around.

2 x 420 g (14¾ oz) tins peach slices in syrup, drained and syrup reserved
400 g (14 oz/2⅔ cups) frozen blueberries, defrosted
2 tablespoons cornflour (cornstarch)
zest and juice of ½ orange
200 g (7 oz) all-butter shortbread biscuits (cookies)
30 g (1 oz/¼ cup) rolled oats
½ teaspoon ground cinnamon
vanilla ice cream, to serve

Preheat the oven to 200°C/180°C Fan/400°F/Gas 6.

Put the peach slices and blueberries into an ovenproof dish, measuring roughly 20 x 30 cm (8 x 12 in). Sprinkle over the cornflour, followed by the orange zest and juice and 3 tablespoons of the reserved peach syrup. Gently toss everything together.

Put the shortbread biscuits into a strong sandwich bag or large bowl. Add the oats and cinnamon, then bash with a rolling pin to an uneven rubble – you want some big pieces and some tiny crumbs.

Sprinkle the shortbread crumble all over the top of the fruit, then drizzle another 3 tablespoons of the peach syrup over the top of the crumble.

Bake for 30 minutes, or until it is crunchy on top and the juices are bubbling up around the edges. Serve hot with vanilla ice cream.

Make ahead

The biscuit topping can be prepped a week in advance. The fruit filling can be made (without cornstarch) 2 hours in advance, if you then stir through the cornstarch before baking.

The shortcut

The freezer and tinned-food aisles of the supermarket are a shortcut cook's best friend   no peeling or chopping required. The shortbread biscuit crumble is also a great-tasting time saver.

Lemon meringue pie

Serves 8
Prep 15 minutes,
plus chilling
Cook 10 minutes

Lemon meringue pie is such a classic, but there are so many points at which failure can occur: weeping meringues, soggy bottoms, runny lemon curd. From the outside you can seemingly have the perfect pie, but slice into it at the wrong moment and you can be faced with a slippery, sliding, not-quite pie more a pool of something that once looked like a pie. My version avoids all of these pitfalls. Firstly, I don't bother making pastry – instead, I use a delicious crunchy biscuit base. Secondly, I buy a jar of lemon curd – no more lemon-flavoured scrambled eggs, no more standing over a bain marie waiting for the all-important curd to appear – simply open a jar! Lastly, my favourite: using the liquid from a can of chickpeas (garbanzo beans), aka aquafaba, to create the best, sweet, sticky pillowy crown.

This is just such a fabulous dessert – it's fun and doesn't take itself seriously. If you love it, try substituting the lemon curd for a dark chocolate ganache – s'mores pie, anyone?

300 g (10½ oz) digestive
biscuits (or Graham crackers)
150 g (5 oz/scant ⅔ cup)
butter, melted
2 x 312 g (11 oz) jar lemon curd
liquid from 400g (14 oz) tin
chickpeas (garbanzo beans)
2 teaspoons cream of tartar
100 g (3½ oz/½ cup) caster
(superfine) sugar

Put the biscuits into a food processor and whizz to form fine crumbs, then add the melted butter and pulse to combine. Alternatively, put the biscuits into a strong sealable plastic bag and bash with a rolling pin, then stir together with the butter in a bowl.

Use the back of a spoon to press the buttery crumbs into the base and sides of a deep 22 cm (8½ in) pie dish or tart tin. Chill in the freezer for 10 minutes.

Remove the base from the freezer and fill with the lemon curd, then chill until ready to serve.

To make the meringue topping, pour the chickpea water (aqua faba) into a large bowl. Add the cream of tartar, then beat the mixture for 10 minutes with an electric whisk. After 5 minutes, gradually add in the sugar, beating after each addition, until the meringue is thick and glossy. Pile the meringue over the lemon curd up to the edge of the crust. Put in the freezer for 20 minutes.

Remove from the freezer and use a cook's blow torch to brown the meringue. Cut into wedges and serve.

Make ahead

+ The base will keep well in the refrigerator for up to 1 week, and can even be made ahead and frozen. Defrost completely before filling.
+ Whip up the meringue and store in the fridge for a few hours. You can assemble when you are ready to serve.

The shortcut

Using aqua faba means you don't have to cook a meringue topping, saving you a good 10 minutes. A jar of store-bought lemon curd saves you a good 30 minutes and a whole lot of lemon scrambled egg anxiety, and a biscuit base versus a pastry base gives you back hours.

Desserts

Dark chocolate pots

Serves 6
Prep 10 minutes

I am blown away by the simplicity of this recipe. Seriously, take a look at the recipe list – you just need chocolate and water! No cream, no egg whites, no whisking egg whites, no worrying about raw egg whites. For me, a bar of good chocolate being the one and only necessity seems like the beginning of a new classic recipe – a recipe I can pretty much rustle up from the bottom of my bag any night of the week.

What I love most about this recipe is that, if it doesn't work out the first time (if, for example, the mixture goes grainy), you can start again. Simply pop the grainy choc back in a pan over a gentle heat and stir until smooth.

These chocolate pots are also super versatile and can be used to top cakes as you would use a ganache. It can also be varied by adding different complementary ingredients, such as orange zest or your favourite boozy tipple.

250 g (9 oz) dark chocolate (minimum 70 percent cocoa solids), finely chopped
175 ml (6 fl oz/¾ cup) just-boiled water
about 12 ice cubes

To serve
handful of toasted salted peanuts, finely chopped (optional)
sweetened whipped cream

Firstly, put the kettle on or heat a pan of water.
Take out two mixing bowls, one larger than the other.
Put the finely chopped chocolate into the smaller bowl and pour over the just boiled water.
Leave to stand for 2 minutes, then gently stir until smooth and very glossy.
Fill the bigger bowl with the ice and set the bowl with chocolate on top. Stir gently until the mixture begins to thicken, once the mixture leaves a thick trail when the spoon is lifted out of the mixture, stop stirring and remove from the ice bath – about 1–2 minutes.
Spoon into serving glasses and sprinkle with chopped salty peanuts and a dollop of sweetened whipped cream.

Make ahead

Finely chop your chocolate and keep it in an airtight (or wandering-greedy-finger-proof) container. Make sure you stock your freezer with a bag of ice.

The shortcut

I'll say it again – chocolate and water. That's all there is to it. You'll never faff with egg whites again.

Free-from carrot cake

Serves 8
Prep 25 minutes, plus
cooling
Cook 30–35 minutes

Nowadays, when you bake a cake for friends, family or work colleagues, it can cause a little panic as you can never be quite sure who's eating what or when. The beauty of this recipe is its infinite adaptability – you can pick and choose your flour, dairy-free milk, nuts, etc., and the recipe will still work and taste great. And the best thing is that you aren't sacrificing any taste or texture by making it free from dairy, gluten and eggs. We are so lucky to be able to get great plant-based alternatives to dairy, and this frosting won't leave you disappointed.

For the cream-cheese -style frosting

75 g (2½ oz/scant ⅓ cup)
dairy-free spread
225 g (8 oz/1½ cups) icing
(confectioner's) sugar
100 g (3 oz/scant ½ cup)
almond milk cream-cheese-
style spread
1 teaspoon vanilla bean paste

For the carrot cake

175 ml (6 fl oz/¾ cup)
light-flavoured oil
175 ml (6 fl oz/¾ cup) dairy-free
milk (I use oat milk)
1 tablespoon cider vinegar
100 g (3½ oz/½ cup) soft light
brown sugar
75 g (2½ oz/⅓ cup) caster
(superfine) sugar
zest of 1 orange
2 teaspoons ground cinnamon
1 teaspoon mixed spice
220 g (8 oz) tin pineapple
chunks, drained
2 carrots (about 180 g/6 oz),
coarsely grated
350 g (12 oz/3 cups) gluten-free
self-raising (self-rising) flour
1 teaspoon bicarbonate of soda
(baking soda)
50 g (2 oz/scant ½ cup) walnut
pieces, plus extra walnuts, finely
chopped, to decorate (optional)
50 g (2 oz/scant ½ cup)
sultanas (golden raisins)

To make the frosting, gently beat the dairy-free spread and icing sugar in a mixing bowl with a wooden spoon until just combined. Gently beat in the cream-cheese-style spread. Do not overbeat or the mixture may split. Cover and chill in the refrigerator until required.

Preheat the oven to 180°C/160°C Fan/350°F/Gas 4. Grease and line the base of two 20 cm (8 in) round cake tins with baking parchment.

In a large jug, beat together the oil, milk, vinegar, both types of sugar, orange zest, spices, pineapple chunks and carrots and a pinch of salt.

Put the flour, bicarbonate of soda, walnuts and sultanas into a large bowl, then add the wet ingredients and stir until completely combined.

Divide the cake batter between the prepared tins and bake for 30–35 minutes or until an inserted skewer comes out clean. Leave to cool in the tins for 5–10 minutes before transferring to a wire rack to cool completely.

Place one cake layer on a serving plate and spread over half of the frosting. Sandwich the second cake layer on top, cover with the remaining frosting and sprinkle over the finely chopped walnuts, if using. Slice and serve.

Make ahead

+ The cake will keep wonderfully, without the frosting, wrapped in cling film (plastic wrap) for up to 3 days, and can be frozen for up to 1 month.
+ The frosting can be made up to 3 days in advance and kept in the refrigerator ready to use.

The shortcut

Why make three desserts to accommodate dietary requirements when you can make a single cake that will make everyone happy?

Desserts

Lemon drizzle cake

Serves 8–10
Prep 10 minutes
Cook 50 minutes–1 hour

Can be frozen

1 x 150 ml (5 fl oz) pot plain yoghurt
1 x yoghurt pot light-flavoured
    oil, plus extra for greasing
2½ x yoghurt pots caster
    (superfine) sugar
3 x yoghurt pots self-raising
    (self-rising) flour
zest and juice of 2 large lemons
3 large eggs

I can always find the time to devour lemon drizzle cake. However, I don't always have the time or inclination to make a cake – what with the measuring and washing up, baking can sometimes seem like a big job. That's why this recipe is so great – it can be whipped up in no time and you don't even have to pull out the kitchen scales. You only use one bowl, one spatula and one loaf pan – is that not the most streamlined cake-making ever?

You do also need a 150 ml (5 fl oz) pot of plain yoghurt – it doubles as your measuring cup, so make sure you don't throw it away in excitement.

I like my lemon drizzle cake zesty and laden with a sweet, tart lemon syrup drizzled generously over the top so it soaks down into the sponge beneath. The combination of yoghurt, oil and all that delicious lemony syrup makes for a moist cake that will keep for several days and is perfect at any time of the day: breakfast made easy with a handful of berries and a dollop of yoghurt; afternoon tea; or a light pud to round off a meal.

This is such a hard-working cake for very little work at all. Enjoy!

Preheat the oven to 180°C/160°C Fan/350°F/Gas 4. Grease and line a 900 g (2 lb) loaf tin (pan) with baking parchment.

Tip the yoghurt into a mixing bowl, then use the empty pot to measure out the 1 pot of oil and 2 pots of sugar, adding them to the bowl. Stir in the 3 pots of flour and the lemon juice and zest and eggs, then beat until combined.

Scrape the cake batter into the prepared tin and bake for 50 minutes–1 hour, or until an inserted skewer comes out clean. If the cake is getting too brown on top, cover loosely with kitchen foil after 30 minutes. Remove to a wire rack to cool in the tin.

While the cake is cooling, make the drizzle. Wash and dry the yoghurt pot, then half-fill with sugar. Add the lemon juice to the pot and stir to combine.

Prick the still-warm cake all over with a skewer or toothpick, then gradually pour the drizzle all over the cake, allowing it to soak in. Allow the cake to cool completely, then remove from the tin and serve in slices.

Make ahead

+ This will keep for at least 3 days, wrapped in cling film (plastic wrap) and stored in an airtight tin.
+ To get the maximum juice from your lemons, give them a 10-second blast in the microwave before squeezing, just before you make the syrup.

The shortcut

Absolutely no time is wasted – no weighing scales, one bowl, one spatula. If there's a faster way to make a lemon drizzle, I'll believe it when I see it.

Desserts

Brownies

Makes   16
Prep   10 minutes
Cook   25 minutes

If, for you, making brownies means grabbing a box from the store and mixing in oil and eggs, then you are going to love this recipe. I started making my brownies with cocoa powder, mostly because it was one of those ingredients I always had in the cupboard, and now I don't make them any other way. I'm in love with the intense chocolate flavour and the dense, fudgy texture.

Gently heating the oil, sugar and cocoa helps to bring the mixture together (no sifting required), but also wakes up the intense chocolatey flavour from within the cocoa powder. (Not to mention filling your kitchen with all sorts of delicious smells.)

These brownies will keep in an airtight container for up to a week and also freeze really well. They are delicious cut into bite-size squares and eaten straight from the freezer like a truffle with a cup of hot coffee.

I like my brownies fudgy and gooey, but if you prefer yours more set, bake for an extra 3–5 minutes.

150 ml (5 fl oz/scant ⅔ cup) light-flavoured oil, plus extra for greasing
250 g (9 oz/generous 1 cup) caster (superfine) sugar
90 g (3¼ oz/¾ cup) cocoa powder (I use 100 percent cocoa solids)
2 teaspoons vanilla extract
¼ teaspoon salt
2 large eggs
50 g (2 oz/generous ⅓ cup) plain (all-purpose) flour

Preheat the oven to 180°C/160°C Fan/350°F/Gas 4. Lightly grease and line a 20 cm (8 in) square baking tin (pan) with baking parchment.

Half-fill a saucepan with water and bring to a gentle simmer over a low heat. Put the oil, sugar, cocoa powder, vanilla and salt into a heatproof bowl and set the bowl over the saucepan pan of barely simmering water. Cook for 3 minutes, stirring frequently. As the mixture gently heats, the ingredients will easily combine until they look glossy. Remove from the heat.

Crack the eggs into the mixture, one at a time, beating really well after each addition until combined – 1–2 minutes. Sprinkle the flour over the surface of the mixture, then beat until no pockets of flour remain.

Scrape the batter into the prepared tin and bake for 20 minutes. Leave to cool in the tin for 10 minutes, then transfer to a wire rack to cool completely. Cut into squares before serving.

Make ahead

The very nature of this recipe is prep ahead, but once you've made them, the brownies will keep in an airtight tin for up to 5 days. Alternatively, they can be frozen for up to 1 month.

The shortcut

No chopping or melting of chocolate, and one less bowl to wash up – that's a good 15 minutes of your life back.

I have many thank yous, firstly dearest Emma Winterschladen who sat next to me on the short train ride, pen in hand and scribbled down my idea for this book whilst I chatted – I somehow just couldn't put the pen to paper myself and our journey helped form the bones of something that turned into this! Thank you Emma, you deserve all the greatness life has to offer you.

To my Aunt Elaine Reynolds who thought this was a great idea and did the first bit of research for me into how non kitchen professionals really do make shortcuts in the kitchen – your pals came up trumps and the information was so insightful and helpful. Your love and support for my work, my books and for me is amazing Elaine, I will always appreciate it.

Thank you to all of the people who tested recipes for me. And to my neighbours who tried, tested and gave invaluable feedback on the food.

Without you Curt this book simply wouldn't exist, you helped me with everything from the first ideas to recipe testing to editing to shopping for ingredients – you're the best and I appreciate you infinitely. You and little A are my world.

Louise Hagger, I've loved your work for so long and it's a privilege to have worked with you on my own book. You and Sophie really worked some magic – thank you!

Jen Kay, your props are beautiful your style is elegant and fun and I love working with you. Thank you for giving so much to this project, you always bring some magic with you.

Troy Willis and Sonali Shah, wow, words cannot express how grateful I am to you guys for helping me in the kitchen on this book and the many others you've cooked next to me. You are both amazing food stylists, cooks, great company and I am truly grateful for your help, support and chat. Thank you.

Evi and Susan this book is a beauty – thank you for your design work.

Emily Preece-Morrison for your editing and finally Eve, you're a wonderful editor and I love working with you; it's so nice that you understand so well what I am trying to do with food! Thank you for letting me make this book.

About the author

Rosie Reynolds is a trained chef, writer and food stylist. She has written cookbooks as well as food styled many best sellers, from *Deliciously Ella* to *Dishoom* and many more. Most importantly, Rosie has written as many recipes as she's had hot dinners, with guest columns in *The Sunday Times* and *The Guardian*. She lives with her partner and baby daughter in London and San Francisco.

Published in 2021 by Hardie Grant Books,
an imprint of Hardie Grant Publishing

Hardie Grant Books (London)
5th & 6th Floors
52–54 Southwark Street
London SE1 1UN

Hardie Grant Books (Melbourne)
Building 1, 658 Church Street
Richmond, Victoria 3121

hardiegrantbooks.com

British Library Cataloguing-in-Publication Data.
A catalogue record for this book is available from the British Library.

The Shortcut Cook by Rosie Reynolds
ISBN: 978-1-78488-351-5

10 9 8 7 6 5 4 3 2 1

Publisher: Kajal Mistry
Commissioning Editor: Eve Marleau
Design: Evi-O.Studio | Susan Le
Photographer: Louise Hagger
Food Stylist: Rosie Reynolds
Prop Stylist: Jennifer Kay
Copy-editor: Emily Preece-Morrison
Proofreader: Tara O'Sullivan
Indexer: Vanessa Bird
Production Controller: Sinead Hering

Colour reproduction by p2d
Printed and bound in China by Leo Paper Products Ltd.